Zero to $10 Million

Zero to $10 Million

How To Build an 8-Figure Technology Business

Shane Brett

BUSINESS EXPERT PRESS

Leader in applied, concise business books

Zero to $10 Million: How To Build an 8-Figure Technology Business

Copyright © Business Expert Press, LLC, 2021.

Cover design by Charlene Kronstedt

Interior design by Exeter Premedia Services Private Ltd., Chennai, India

First published in 2021 by
Business Expert Press, LLC
222 East 46th Street, New York, NY 10017
www.businessexpertpress.com

ISBN-13: 978-1-95334-968-2 (paperback)
ISBN-13: 978-1-95334-969-9 (e-book)

Business Expert Press Entrepreneurship and Small Business Management Collection

Collection ISSN: 1946-5653 (print)
Collection ISSN: 1946-5661 (electronic)

First edition: 2021

10 9 8 7 6 5 4 3 2 1

Dedication

I would like to dedicate this book to:

- Conor & Darragh—My beautiful boys & best buddies for life.
- Ciara—For 20 years or adventure, love, and happiness
  We miss you every day.
- Dad—For making me the man I am today in every way.
- Neil—For being the best brother ever. I see you every time my boy's smile.
- Mam—I miss our chats so much. Look after Neil for me.
- Sean and Dympna—For being the best in-laws on the planet.
- Catherine—For the years of friendship and support during the hardest year of my life.
- Emil—For being the best business mentor ever. Land and expand buddy!
- Simon & Graham—For being the best friends I guy could have.
- Porkpie—Pete, Mickey & Mick for being the best bandmates ever.
- Marian—For making me happy again. I am so excited about our future together.

Description

Zero to $10 Million is a practical step by step guide that teaches entrepreneurs' how to build a $10 million dollar technology business. It describes in detail how to create a great product, find a brilliant team, raise money from professional investors, and then scale the company globally.

It is what works in the "real world".

This book is written by Shane Brett—a serial technology entrepreneur with many years' experience of setting up, funding, and scaling technology start-ups worldwide. It follows the exact steps and processes he used to reach a $10 million dollar valuation and raise multiple rounds of funding from venture capital investors.

The text is perfect for aspiring entrepreneurs, budding founders, and anyone who wants to understand how to build a successful technology start-up from the ground up. It breaks down the mystery behind how to grow a new technology business and explains what it is actually like to be a start-up CEO and how to manage the daily challenges and constant stress.

Keywords

start-up; entrepreneur; software; technology; venture capital; fundraising; seed funding round; series a funding; angel investment; fintech; founder; resilience

Contents

Introduction

Why I Wrote This Book

This is the book I wanted to read when I was starting out—and I could not find it anywhere.

When I was setting up my technology company, there was no practical, step-by-step guide to reaching Series A funding.

This book is the new playbook for business founders to reach that important milestone.

It is a detailed start-up guide to taking the correct steps to attain an eight-figure valuation in under three years. It has been tried and tested and follows the exact template and processes I used to reach that point with my own technology business.

Many of the existing start-up books I devoured in my early days were by wealthy investors, ivory tower academics, or members of the "Silicon Valley Boys Club."

I did not want that. I needed "Real World" advice on how to build a new product, find an awesome team, put a great pitch deck together, find fantastic clients, and raise millions of dollars in seed capital. I needed something I could dip into and digest quickly. A book that understood that my funds were limited, and I also had a family to support, with limited financial means to make a success of the company.

This book fills that gap.

It breaks down the mystery behind how to set up, fund, and scale a technology business.

It doesn't tell you theoretically what you should do. It tells you exactly what I did to reach a $10 million dollar valuation.

Growing a new technology start-up follows a well-established pattern—one I didn't know existed when I started out. This book brings structure to that pattern.

It explains what it is actually like to be a start-up CEO. How to manage the daily challenges and constant stress. It identifies when you should start speaking to seed investors, how to market your product, and then find initial clients. It explains how institutional funding works, when to target larger companies and how to set the business up to reach Series A funding.

There is a template underlying the path from Day 1 of a new business to reaching a $10 million dollar valuation. For the first time, this book documents these processes, lifts the lid on the steps to take, explains what adds the most value, what will work, and what won't. It explains how to overcome the constant roadblocks and knockbacks you will experience along the way.

The "struggle" of the start-up CEO is like nothing else in business. The endless grind wears most entrepreneurs down. The challenge of trying to keep your personal life on track and the business solvent is too much for most people. And with good reason. The pressure goes on every day for years and it often happens while your funding is running out, payroll is approaching, suppliers are screaming to be paid, and existing clients are getting cranky.

Everyone knows setting up a business is backbreaking work and incredibly stressful. This book will help alleviate some of that stress by breaking down what you need to do, when you need to do it, and how to successfully move to the next stage of company growth.

When I was considering starting a company, I searched hard for a detailed, real life, practical guide explaining how to build a new technology business from scratch. One that was written by someone who had actually done it and was aimed at a new entrepreneur that had never worked in the technology industry before but had ambitions to scale the business globally.

It took me five years to build a company from nothing to being offered a Series A funding deal at a valuation of $10 million dollars. I honestly believe I could have done it in half that time if I had known what's in this book.

I wasted months, even years in some cases, going down the wrong route for funding, targeting the wrong initial clients, and building the wrong products—simply because I didn't know any better.

The entrepreneur's journey is a fantastically rewarding one—you are trying to create new wealth out of nothing but brain power—an idea in your head.

There is a series of key steps and developments that need to take place to grow your new idea into an eight-figure valuation. This book provides the guide to reaching that milestone.

This is what works in the "Real World."

How the Book Is Structured

This book is structured over a **typical three-year period** from the very first start-up steps, right through to securing a Series A funding deal. While it focuses on technology company start-ups and those that sell software to business customers, the lessons and suggestions in here are applicable to any new start-up business globally.

Part I of the book focuses on typical business activities in year one. This includes setting the business up, building an initial version of your product, and finding the first couple of team members you will need to grow the company. It also covers how to market the new business successfully, while managing cash flow to ensure the company does not go bankrupt in that challenging first year.

Part II moves onto year two. It covers how to find and implement your first real business client and how to begin the process of identifying suitable investors. It explains the typical angel and seed funding process and looks at how to find great "trusted advisors" (e.g., accountants, lawyers) to help you scale the business quickly.

Part III covers year three. This includes the personal resilience you will need to keep successfully growing the company over many years. This includes how to sell the product to large organizations and then how to maintain innovating, while scaling your company globally and securing Series A funding at a valuation in excess of $10 million.

PART I

CHAPTER 1

Turning an Idea Into a Company

Solve Your Own Problem

Find out what annoys you and start thinking about a solution to fix it. It's as simple as that.

If something drives you crazy, it's likely to annoy a lot of people too. And companies will pay you money if you solve it. If there is no obvious solution for this problem, then you could have found a great business idea.

You will likely have been working for a while, perhaps even for many years. This means you know an industry particularly well. You know the pain points and what doesn't work and have a network of colleagues and friends throughout that market.

You have probably thought many times how new or better technology could really boost an organization's efficiency or reduce costs. Start thinking about what that technology would look like. Ask your peers what really bothers them. What their dream solution would contain. What would be needed to make it work globally.

Every one of us has a bunch of problems that they encounter every day that could be solved with the right technology. Solve your own problem and you might have the first step toward a successful business.

My Story

I worked in London for years. After the 2008 financial crisis, I set up a consultancy to advise fund companies on how to implement mountains of new regulation and compliance rules they were having to adopt. It was a headache. The fund managers hated it. It was really expensive and there was no obvious benefit (in their eyes). I was trying to manage massive global compliance projects taking place under rock-hard regulatory deadlines with huge fines and negative publicity if they weren't completed on time.

We were trying to manage all of these fund compliance projects on spreadsheets. It was a complete and utter disaster.

I looked valiantly and with an open check book to try and buy specific software to bring some order to the chaos. I couldn't find it anywhere. One major financial institution even offered to pay for it for their project. But it wasn't possible. The software didn't exist. The last really big project I managed was so stressful and so chaotic that I decided I would not run another global regulatory fund project without having suitable software.

I found lots of generic project management software available, but they were of no use to the investment management community. I needed a fund management specific compliance solution to manage the specificities of the industry and make sense of the regulatory madness.

So, I saved the money I had made from compliance consulting and moved back to Ireland, where I started to build it.

I knew I couldn't manage any more projects without proper software and I knew from listening to half my industry complain about this issue that many were in the same boat and—crucially—would pay for a good solution to make their lives easier.

The Best Person for the Job

It makes it much easier to grow your business and raise money later if you are a **Subject Matter Expert** ("SME") in your industry. That is, you know the space inside out. If you are a chemist who wants to automate a drug testing process, if you are a civil engineer who wants to manage a bridge construction or if you are a vet who wants to develop a new animal registration database—all the aspects of growing your software company will be made **much** easier by you being an expert in your field.

However, it is even better if, while also being an expert on your industry, that you are also a recognized **leader** in your field, that is, a "Thought Leader" in your niche and known for it. This is important because it means you can't get caught out easily with questions from potential clients and investors. You are a known entity in this area. You have credibility and a great reputation. This means you have a strong chance of getting in the door of companies you know well and the solution you build will be taken seriously by them. This makes you a much more credible future investment opportunity when you start to look for funding.

Best of all worlds is that you are an expert in your field, recognized in your industry as a thought leader *and* **you have a wide network.** It is absolutely **crucial** for an expanding successful technology start-up to have a readymade professional network to market the product to. They can also provide feedback and research, help design the solution, and then finally, become the first business customers. How are you going to get your product in front of the right people in the right companies if you don't know them and they don't know you?

There are ways around this (and we will cover that in the marketing chapter), but it slows everything down. And for business to business sales, that means years to make a successful high figure sale—not months or weeks.

If you haven't got a great social media following and do not speak at industry conferences and events, or even publish blog posts, then this is going to be a problem. Start changing this right now.

Non-technology Software Founders

You have probably never run a tech company before. That is fine. I had not either. I did not know a line of code from a jar of coffee. I still don't know much about coding, and I don't care to ever learn. You do not need to understand programming languages to build a tech business. You need to understand customer pain points, how software can take their pain away, and what benefits the user needs to attain from your solution.

Start-Up Essentials

In this initial setup chapter, we will cover the following kick off essentials:

1. Initial funds
2. Legal

3. Logistics

4. First company deck

5. Pitching the business

Initial Funds

To kick this thing off, you are going to need at least $30,000. Ideally, you should have $130,000, but that's probably not a realistic option for most people. $30,000 is an amount that is possible for many people to save or borrow and it's more importantly also a reasonable amount to build a decent "Minimum Viable Product" (MVP) of your solution. It won't deliver a completed enterprise (i.e., large company) ready software solution, but it should allow you to build a first version that covers the main pain points you are solving and excite the interest of your industry.

Legal

Set up your company right now. It can be daunting and frightening taking this real and tangible first step—but it separates 90 percent of the great idea merchants from the actual "Doers."

Remember, ideas are ten a penny—the gold is in implementing them and that is what you are going to do now.

That pain you experience in registering the company in your location and the setting up of online tax accounts are all parts of making this real. Investors will expect it and so will your first clients.

Remember—before you incorporate, you are an idea. After you incorporate, you are a **real entity**.

One that exists in the "Real World" and one that you can now grow and add value to, as you begin your journey to an eight-figure valuation.

Logistics

Where are you going to be located? That is a key question but not one you need to resolve right now. In the age of flexible start-up space, you can use your bedroom in one of the innumerable start-up hubs in every major global city.

If you opt to keep things from home initially as you get your MVP developed, at the very least, spend a couple of hundred dollars a month getting a business address from a respected business hub. That way, you can get business cards printed that are credible and you can update your business e-mail signature with your office location (see below). All of this makes you look like a real company.

If at all possible, set up the business in a location close to but cheaper than a major business center. That way, you can attract employees with good experience but a shorter commute and lower cost of living, while at the same time, allowing you to easily service business clients not that far away. In the post-pandemic world this may also make the company more attractive to future employees.

You will not be able to compete with the salaries large companies pay for many years. Don't let that worry you too much. Large companies are boring. What you can compete with is flexible working conditions in an exciting start-up environment and a great quality of life.

I set up my technology company one hour from downtown Dublin in Ireland. This meant easy access to the main North/South motorway on the island and 40 minutes from one of Europe's busiest airports, with a flight to London every fifteen minutes and direct nonstop services to Dubai, Hong Kong, and hundreds of weekly flights to the United States, New York, and San Francisco. It was also much, much cheaper than trying to locate in Dublin or London city center (our annual rental first year was less than $4,000).

Investigate if there are any government or local incentives to help you set up. In some countries, these can be substantial and the cash flow in the early days is invaluable. You are likely starting a business in advanced or emerging technology. Every country in the world would like these types of businesses in their backyard. They are the future of employment and one of the growth trends in the global economy.

Speak to the **government start-up body and the local Chamber of Commerce**. Grants may be available, as well as financial support for creating high quality jobs, tax breaks for new businesses, and even free assistance from local higher educational institutes. The support we had in the first couple of years was invaluable to staying afloat.

Now go into your local bank with your company registration documents and **set up a business bank account.** Deposit your start-up capital and ask for a debit card. You are now ready to begin trading. Pity it will probably be at least a year before there is any revenue coming in. But don't worry. For "Business to Business" (B2B) start-ups, this is normal. You just need to stay alive long enough to get there.

Set up the company e-mail and website. E-mail set up is a simple step but an important one. Get your company e-mail set up so it's clear you are not just a small operator with limited vision and plans. So, if your company is called "Colonize the Moon" your e-mail should be "Shane@ colonizethemoon.com". I recommend using a Google Gmail business account for this. It's easy to set up and reasonably priced, both initially and as you expand and add more staff and users. Also, set up a second "info" e-mail account that is forwarded to your main company account. This will make your business look larger than it is.

These days, there are many lovely **template websites** that you can use to create a nice professional looking website in a weekend with no coding experience required. You only need a few pages initially. A section about the company, the product you are building, and you as founder.

Complete some secondary **market research** into the opportunity you are targeting. This will enhance your own primary experience of the industry and the problem you are trying to solve. Have a few cups of coffee or Zoom meetings with people from companies in the space (and hopefully, who you know), to get their thoughts and another viewpoint on your proposed solution. This can be very enlightening, and it expands your network.

Many start-up gurus suggest a very expansive and detailed round of market research, but the good news is, if you are solving your own problem and know the industry very well, this research is more for validation.

You now need to think about pulling together some sort of **first version of your solution**. You are going to need someone to do it. I am taking it for granted it's not going to be you. An entrepreneur with the coding skills to build an enterprise product, is very rarely the same person as the CEO of the company who will design the product, find the team, procure the clients, and secure the funding you need to grow this business. It's a completely different set of skills.

So, you will need to find the right person or company to build the first MVP. That process is covered in detail in the next chapter. Jot your initial ideas into a document and you can use this to populate the product page of your first company presentation (see below). This will be expanded later to provide a clear and illustrated walkthrough of your new product and the key features it should contain.

This first MVP will be a long way from the product you deploy with business client number one, but it's another key first step along the way. Forget about advanced bells and whistles for the moment and concentrate on trying to build a 3 wheeled car. You can add the 4th wheel in later iterations.

First Company Deck

Don't worry about a business plan for the moment. You can get to that later in the first year, when you start actively looking for funding. Let this book be your business plan for the first few months.

The key thing—and you should spend some time on this—is pulling together an **initial company presentation** (called a "deck"), which you can send far and wide and share with everyone who takes an interest in your new venture (and even those who don't).

This deck will become your **initial core piece of company collateral** in those first months, while you work on building an MVP of your product. You will need to learn it backwards and be able to pitch it till you are blue in the face.

The deck will contain:

- The problem you have identified
- The solution you will provide
- The team you will assemble
- The size of the potential market
- The key steps you have already taken
- The future steps you will take this year
- The funding you will need next to make it happen

This deck will take many iterations and as you present it more and more, it will be refined to address questions you are asked from interested parties, potential team members, clients, and particularly investors.

Deck Structure

The front page should have an initial logo for your business (large size) and a tagline for who you are going to be, for example, "Colonize the Moon Inc.—Bringing Lunar travel to the masses."

Whatever. It's just a starting point and can be updated as you hone your message and company identity. Similarly, almost any symbol at all for a logo will work at this stage.

The format should be approximately 10 slides in total (excluding the front page). Any more than that and people's eyes glaze over and they will lose interest.

Remember the old Silicon Valley Rule of Thumb here—**10/20/30.**

Your deck should consist of 10 slides that take no more than 20 minutes to present (ideally, a lot less) and with type written in 30 size fonts.

That's a good rule of thumb to live by. Very few investors will ask you to make your deck or your presentation longer. Most want 10 minutes max—or even five minutes. In the United States, two-minute pitches are common. The aim is a brief summary of what you are about.

One Irish "Venture Capital" (VC) investor I know sits through approximately seven hundred pitches like this every year. They normally invest in about twelve. So, your deck needs to be in the format they are used to seeing and containing the information they expect.

You can also use this deck to prepare shortened summaries of who you are and what you want. Opportunities like this occur all the time at business events, industry presentations, and at the sidebar of a conference. Get to know it off by heart. You will be pitching it endlessly over the next few months.

While this first deck will contain the same core detail, you will find yourself chopping and changing it to suit your audience and occasion. It will be revised and updated constantly, as the company sharpens its strategic focus and you find product/market fit.

At my company, we went through at least six branding changes, multiple name changes, and strategic pivots over the first two years while we got established and put our angel funding in place.

Think of this presentation like your CV or resume. You probably have a core resume that contains every great thing you have ever done. It's likely that when you apply for a job you want, you review it and cut and chop bits out, and then put it together to suit the position you want. It is the exact same mindset with your initial company deck. Chop and change it to suit the investors, prospects, or partners that will see it.

PowerPoint is fine to use (if a bit chunky on memory) and Google Slides is a good option too.

The structure of your initial company deck should be as follows:

1. **Problem**—Succinctly summarize the core issue that is driving everyone crazy—for example, "Why can't we holiday on the Moon safely?"
2. **Solution**—In bright large letters, make it clear what the industry needs to fix this problem—for example, what the space industry needs is a new technology solution to make lunar travel safe and inexpensive.
3. **Product**—Explain how your amazing new product will fix this problem. For example, "We are building the first healthy and safe software solution for lunar travel." Also include a picture of your solution here. Of course, it's not built yet right? So, grab something off the Internet (preferably royalty free) that looks like what you are planning to build and add in a few changes to cover the specific great functionality you will deploy.

   At this stage, the product slide can be quick and dirty. You can add more to this in the future. This is for a talking point at this stage only. Everyone knows you are only out of the starting gate and your product is evolving. The important thing—the really important thing—is to have the vision and the implementation skills to be able to deliver it. That's the difference between a million failed start-up's and one that becomes the Series A success.
4. **Team**—Add three or four photos with names and occupation beneath. By all means, stick in another short line of experience (e.g., 15 years at Google, etc.). But keep this concise. Of course, your team may just be you. It will nearly certainly be missing a few of the key people you need to hire to get the company off the ground. That's ok. People expect this. It's important you have identified the positions you will need to hire. Where there are gaps, put a question mark in each missing photo and explain who they are going to

be. For example, below one empty picture you could put "Head of Engineering - shortlist identified. Offer to be made when funding confirmed."

5. **Size of the market**—Include a ballpark estimation on the current market size for your product and the potential future growth over the next few years. Don't put silly numbers like $40 trillion and so on. That is not realistic and makes you look like an amateur. The key thing is to look at the **potential *addressable* market**—particularly over the next 24 to 36 months. What good is it to you if your most likely target clients are copper miners in Chile and you are located a dozen time zones away in Dubai. For my company, we knew there were 3,000 fund managers globally and that each of them was spending an average of $2 million a year on compliance and that number was growing all the time. The large ones were spending many multiples of this. They had both the pain and the budget to spend money on a solution software to take their compliance headache away.

Note that all this market data and information was easily available online. If you can't find it for your industry, then you are not trying hard enough. If it's a genuinely new space, make an informed and reasonable guesstimate. You will be ripped to shreds by professional investors if you put down ridiculous numbers.

6. **How you will make money?**—This is obviously key. Many end user applications like the kind of consumer apps Silicon Valley specializes in (Facebook, LinkedIn, Twitter, etc.) had the revenue come after user growth. That is, they spent a fortune to build a user base first. Amazon spent a few billion dollars even before making any profit. You are not Amazon and you are (likely) not in Silicon Valley. You don't have the same connections in Palo Alto or on Sand Mill road. You live back here in the "Real World."

That method of scaling is not going to work because you will be out of money long before your customer acquisition gets anywhere near the revenue or retention rate you need to be profitable (or investable).

Give up on that idea, and instead, put down three sources of revenue from your software clients. In this example, I am presuming it's a B2B business.

The three examples are:

1. **Core User License Fee**—The fee that each client will pay to use the solution. There are a million ways to slice and dice this number (see the chapter on Pricing).
2. **Support**—Once the business is established, you may be able to charge customers for extended business hour coverage outside their core time zone.
3. **Consulting and customization**—Clients will often ask for some specific development work and there may be an opportunity to use your Subject Matter Expertise to provide some consulting to customers. Most professional investors would not like to see consulting revenue to be more than 20 percent of your expected total revenue. They want to see repeatable fee income, not one-off consulting work.

VC investors want to see long term contracts in place of recurring monthly license fees (with a minimum pricing floor) and upward only pricing reviews, as your solution expands out to different teams across a global business.

That's the goal. But it will take time to get there. Consulting is good for cashflow the first couple of years but the difference to your valuation can be stark. A recurring license fee contract typically adds triple the value to your "Pre-Money Valuation" (i.e., pre-investment company value), compared to a one off or likely but non contractually recurring piece of work.

7. **Initial traction**—This is another important slide. What have you done to date? Who have you spoken to (even over coffees)? What feedback have you received? What funding have you applied for? What demonstrable steps have you taken to turn this idea into a reality?

For example, you could state that your MVP was in its second iteration, you have applied for government research funding, you have had multiple initial meetings with potential future prospects, and that you have "established relationships" (always a good vague term) with a number of potentially interesting future partners. You are going to be asked a lot of questions about what you have written here, so make sure everything has that core kernel of truth and a potentially extremely exciting upside. This is CV inflation for start-ups.

8. **Plans from here**—What are you going to do next? Put down three bullet points for the next quarter, the rest of the year and the strategy for next year. Make these difficult but achievable. This quarter could be to finish and test the MVP. Rest of the year could be used to launch a paid pilot with a first interested client. Next year, it could be to secure seed funding, expand the team and target the first overseas customer. All these plans should reflect your real strategy, but from the perspective of an investor, that is, how will your plans rapidly increase the valuation of the company.

   Remember, an investor is putting their money behind you and your team every bit as much as behind your product and idea. At this stage, it is the quality, experience, and motivation of the founder and initial hires that can mean the difference between an investor writing a check and sitting on the fence.

9. **Funding requirements**—How much money are you going to need this year and the next to turn this project into a thriving business? State that you are looking for $50,000 to $100,000 angel funding immediately to fund the business for the next twelve months and get the first client signed up and onboarded.

   I can tell you right now that you will need a **lot** more than that. Likely in excess of half and probably closer to a million dollars seed round in due course. Don't worry about that right now. A promise of adding a lot of value to the company for a relatively small amount of angel capital is enticing for potential investors.

10. **Wrap up slide**—This is a simple wrap up slide with four bullet points covering the name of the company, the problem you are addressing, how you will solve it and most importantly—your "Ask." Always include an "Ask" at the end of every presentation. Some companies ask for nonfinancial favors (e.g., introductions to potential clients or employees). I don't expect that to be you. Instead, you will likely be running out of funding as we speak. Ask for investment. At this stage, that's the $50,000 angel we discussed earlier. Have a good answer ready for what you plan to do with that kind of money—and

of course, the answer is to finalize building the product and start to hire some staff. Early stage angel investors don't like to see the founder taking much salary at the early stage.

Later formats of this core deck can be refined to expand on the product, for initial customer prospects, and potential investors. It can expand on what funds you plan to raise and how you will spend it (for potential investors). Other interested third parties will want to know more about the company itself (think regulators, service providers including lawyers, and accountants) and potential company advisors.

You are going to be presenting this deck repeatedly in this first year. Get to know it inside out. Anticipate answers to the questions you will learn to expect. Update it constantly with ideas that come to you in the night and with feedback you receive from the listeners.

Pitching the Business

You will be pitching the company to investors, potential clients, prospective employees, and hopefully at industry events. Lots of them. Get used to it. If you hate public speaking, you will have to overcome this, or you won't make it far with the business.

If you haven't pitched much before, watch as many great business presentations as you can online. How do the speakers talk? How do they walk? Where do they leave gaps and pauses? How do they move their hands and arms? Great pitching is an art, but the good news is that it can be easily learnt with practice.

When you pitch, remember that **you** are the presentation. Your deck should not be the focus of your presentation. You are an entrepreneur not a college lecturer.

Your deck is the **"wallpaper"** to your presentation. This advice is so essential to fundraising, I am going to state it again—your deck is the wallpaper—**you** are the presentation.

You must take this advice on board if you ever hope to raise any money from professional investors.

If you read off your deck or if it's covered in tons of writing, then no one listens to you anyway. They just read the deck while you are talking.

Your whole pitch, all the work you spent putting into the presentation, all the research, all your practicing is wasted and the first impression you will make on anyone is boredom or even worse.

You would not believe the number of entrepreneurs that get this wrong.

Consider your deck to be the essential "talking points" of your presentation—not your presentation.

Do a good pitch and you are in the top 20 percent of entrepreneurs looking for funding that an average VC is seeing.

VCs are like film critics having to watch fifty versions of "Attack of the Killer Tomatoes" to find that one "Reservoir Dogs."

You can be Mr. White. Practice your pitch. Do it in front of your team. Take feedback and do it again. Then make them drill you (with likely and hard questions), and finally, allow thirty seconds longer than the time you think it will take. For some unknown reason, pitching live always takes a little longer than you expect from rehearsals. You don't want to be the idiot who gets the bell rung before their great finale and gets booted off the stage. It happened to me once in San Francisco many years ago. It was such a mortifying experience, it hasn't happened to me since.

Conclusion

Great. Now your company exists. You have business cards printed, a decent website, and e-mail set up, as well as a first deck to extol the virtues of your new enterprise to all and sundry. You have even started working on your first MVP and will have something to demo soon.

Congratulations. You have now done more than 90 percent of what every aspiring entrepreneur talks about doing.

You are now in the top 10 percent.

Chapter Summary

- Establish yourself as a respected Thought Leader in your industry.
- Incorporate the company.
- Open a bank account for the business.

- Complete some primary and secondary market research on the opportunity.
- Start formulating what the first version of your MVP will look like.
- Decide where to locate.
- Investigate local and government start-up incentives.
- Set up company e-mail and website.
- Build a good first company deck and refine it constantly.
- Practice pitching the deck repeatedly and update it with feedback and answers to the questions you are asked.

CHAPTER 2

Building a Product

Introduction

Many start-up and business books recommend building a great team first and then working on a fast/failure model of product development.

In the "Real World," that won't work.

You won't have the start-up capital to hire the team you need or the time to do it.

Maybe the "team first" model works in Silicon Valley, where people will often work initially for free (called "sweat equity") and entrepreneurs with a good deck get funded for millions of dollars. However, back here in the "Real World," you need to have at least something exciting and dynamic to show as a product, before anyone sane is going to consider leaving Facebook or Google or their Academic cushion to come and work for you and your little pipedream.

So, by all means, start conversations with the folks you would like to have on your team in due course, but immediately on Day 1 of your business starting, get going on building an initial version of your product. While building your team is obviously key to turning your idea into a scalable business, it's much better to have something concrete to show people. Even if it's just some iterations of a "Wireframe" and initial MVP.

A **Wireframe** is a sketched out "Mock-up" of the key pages on each screen of your software. They clearly show the buttons, options, actions, and visual representation that the end user will see. They are super helpful both for your developers to use as a template for the first build and for you as the designer. It helps you think critically about the user workflow and how the users will interact with the technology you are building. Your solution can have all the amazing functionality in the world, but if it's hard for clients to use or doesn't make sense to them or the industry, then you are wasting your time and your money.

By all means, draft a Wireframe if you yourself are able to. These are easy to complete and great for visualizing your vision to developers. Ask a tech friend to help you if needs be. Not the developer of your product (you need to be able to fire them). There are tons of free Wireframe websites and apps available online to get you started (or visit my website shanebrett.io).

An MVP is a **Minimum Viable Product**, that is, developing an initial product with the minimum features required in it to be of use to an initial client and user. The budget for building a good MVP you can demo to a client should be below $30,000.

Larger companies pay millions to develop enterprise software. You don't have to. You are fast and nibble. You know your industry segment. You know the leading players, and most importantly, you know the pain they are experiencing. You can build something in a few months that will start providing the solution.

Once the business is set up, you should complete the following product development steps:

1. **Pulling together the initial funds for your MVP**—This will be either the start-up funding you have saved, perhaps a government grant, or a loan from a bank or third party. I don't recommend taking family money. Not unless you want every future Christmas/Thanksgiving dinner to (probably) be a very tense affair.
2. **Designing the MVP**—Initial research with target market could just be yourself and a few trusted peers.
3. **Finalizing your MVP development**—You should aim to complete two rounds of product development. This is key. The initial MVP you receive and then the updated MVP will enable you to get detailed feedback on what works and what needs to be added. Then, when you have incorporated them into your updated MVP, you should be ready to show it to potential customers.

Getting Started on your Minimum Viable Product (MVP)

You will need to find the right person or company to build version 1.0. The secret here is to ask around. Ask your friends in software. Mine your professional network for recommendation and then look for references from a couple of developers. If you know any other technology entrepreneurs, they should be at the top of your list.

This first MVP will be a long way from the product you deploy with your first client, but it's another key first step. Forget about the ideal end solution right now and instead focus on the core key benefits you want to provide your client.

You are aiming to have something good and that is ready to get people excited for under thirty thousand dollars. Ideally, closer to twenty thousand dollars if possible. In this age of open source code and fast product development, this should be achievable.

Obviously, you have to make sure in black and white that the intellectual property belongs to your company and not the product developer. Make sure you can see that clearly in any contract or document before giving the green light and paying an initial mobilization fee.

Many product developers will look for half the money upfront. That's ok, but it's not ideal for you. If possible, negotiate hard for one third upfront, one third on initial delivery, and the final third after your feedback and changes have been added to the MVP. This will give you more leverage and power in the development process.

Also, make it clear to the developers that this is just an initial piece of work and if they do a good job and you establish a working relationship, then there will be a lot of follow on work as part of a long term business partnership.

Regardless of how the commercials are structured, you must make sure the deal is agreed on a flat fee basis—not on a per day or with any variable element. You can't afford that, and it will kill your cash flow quickly. If the project is for a set fee, then the developers will be keen to deliver it quickly, get your approval, finalize any updates, and move onto their next project.

If at all possible—and this goes for all aspects of your business—try and meet the developer/development company face to face once. Of course this may not be easy, given geographical locations and the recent pandemic, but business flows so much smoother when you have met in person before.

As the product evolves, you will need to expand the product pages of your first deck to provide a clear, illustrated walkthrough of our new product and the key features it will contain.

Using MoSCoW Prioritization

To decide on what needs to go into this first iteration of your MVP, try using the **MoSCoW** prioritization methodology. **MoSCoW** stands for must have, should have, could have, and won't have. Every idea you have had in relation to the new technology needs to be dropped into one of these buckets.

To do this, think carefully and critically about your new software product and what needs to go in there right now to catch the interest of your first client.

"Must have"—are critical requirements. There is no way around these requirements. They are crucial to the product's success. It is essential that these pieces of functionality are ready to use in your product right from Day 1. Without them in there from the get-go, no one will buy the product because it won't solve the problem it's meant to address. These items must go into your first MVP right now and should be reflected in any Wireframe mock-up immediately.

"Should have"—are important but not necessary. Ideally, they would be in the product if time and money allowed. Often, they can be time dependent, that is, a nice report or new drop-down menu that should definitely be in there but due to your delivery deadline, will have to wait till the next build. If you know your industry well, you will probably spend more time considering what "Should" be in there versus what you know "Must" be in your Day 1 product.

"Could have"—are desirable but not necessary. These developments could improve the user experience and make your clients happier and probably would not cost much in additional time or budget (e.g., more options in a particular field). These are up for discussion with your development team if time and resources permit. "Could haves" have a question mark over them with the development team, as they need to be validated as to whether or not they are easy to build.

"Won't have"—are not going to be built right now. What could this be? I hear you say. Often this will be something that is just not possible at the current phase of development (and often for the foreseeable future). You know clients will want it further down the line and it may very well be required eventually, but right now, it's beyond the scope of your budget and timetable. For example, an advanced reporting module may be a certain requirement for you to successfully deploy the solution globally at a large company. The problem is that you could spend a couple of million dollars on this enhancement alone, so it will have to wait till later. Any questions from prospects about these kinds of requirements should be met with: "It's one of the items we are considering for our future Product Roadmap."

Most decent MVPs will consist of a large number of **Must haves**, a few important nice to have **Should haves,** and potentially a couple of **Could haves,** if your development team think they are easy to deploy.

There is a lot of more interesting information about the **MoSCoW** prioritization method of software development available online.

Product Development Document

Before commissioning the MVP, you will need to prepare a "Product Development Document" for the developers. This document will scope out the details of what is required on each screen, how the user will interact with each, and how they will relate to each other. This walk-through document must cover each of the main screens on the product. It will be the guiding light of development, so document everything carefully.

This document should be structured as follows:

- An **introduction** explaining the business case, for example, this software solution will be used by the health and safety department of lunar transport companies to manage passenger health readiness for travel into orbit.
- Explain **each screen** in the application. A wireframe screen shot of each is ideal. Then, an explanation below the picture outlining what each piece of functionality (e.g., Drop down, Button, Click-box, etc.) should do.

- Explain how they will **relate to each other**, for example, if I click this button at the top of screen X, it takes me to screen Y.
- Outline how the user is expected to **interact** with the software, for example, a typical user will review the data in screen X and click a "checkbox when complete" box. This will then take them to Screen Y where they can run a simple report.

If you are trying to build a new product for an industry or area that you have little experience in, this is where you will come unstuck. Your requirements will be mere guesses. You won't know what people will buy, never mind what will sell. The key "Must haves" and "Should haves" won't be correct. You will have built the wrong MVP and then you are out of cash.

Managing the Development Cycle

This is probably the first time you have managed a software development process and it may be particularly fraught, as you are likely using your own hard-earned cash, so you need to end up with something good.

Developers can be hard to manage. Treat this initial development process as good practice for managing your team later, as the company expands.

The best approach is one of constructive collaboration. Jumping up and down doesn't work (as you will find out). Emphasize the long-term relationship you are keen to build. Be friendly and polite. Use external deadlines as a driver to keep things on track (i.e., I am demoing this at a conference on the 15th of next month; the first prospect wants to see it in six weeks and so on).

Send them the wireframe and the Product Development Document you have drafted. Give them a day or two to review it and then have a detailed call walking through each part of the document and answering any questions they will have (developers always have loads). Feel free to grab screenshots of other software layouts that you like and send it to them for guidance.

Agree to a follow-on call each Friday (or Monday) to agree the work schedule and for them to update you on what has been built (ideally showing you) and to decide on the next stage of the product development. This meeting just needs to be twenty minutes. Keep it brief and constructive.

Finalizing a Good MVP

It's going to take two rounds of development (minimum) to get your MVP close to what you envisaged.

The first delivery will be the initial draft. What the developers have understood from your Product Development Document. They should be able to deliver a Version 1.0 of the MVP in six to eight weeks (ideally less).

The commercial agreement with them needs to include this second round of development. Otherwise, it can get awfully expensive and you can be left with a useless product.

When the developers deliver Version 1.0, have them arrange a "Review Meeting" a few days later to walk you through their development and their logic behind each screen. You need to be fully **ready** for this.

Use the few days in between delivery and the Review Meeting to play with Version 1.0. Try and break it. Take loads of notes and get lots of questions ready. This is your chance to make sure you are happy and ask for any changes (there will be plenty).

Carefully reconcile what has been delivered to what you requested in the Product Development Document. Note any differences or required changes. Document what you are not happy with and the changes you suggest versus the changes you are insisting upon.

The first development phase will have given you a chance to think about any additional functionality or changes that are required. This second iteration of the MVP is based on your feedback as a Subject Matter Expert in your industry and perhaps suggestions from the first parties who have seen the initial wireframe mock-up.

Your satisfaction with the second iteration of your MVP should be wholly driven by what you know you can **sell** in your industry. Is this version 2.0 enticing enough to be of interest to potential prospects? Can you comfortably demo the MVP to a room full of strangers?

Demoing software is an art in itself and one that only comes after months (years!) of experience. (See Chapter 6.) Demoing can be hard to get right until you do it. Get started as soon as possible.

Start Looking for Feedback

Now that you have spent your hard-earned cash, hopefully you have something exciting to show for it. It won't be perfect and will be a long way from your ideal product, but it should be dynamic enough to demonstrate the flavor and potential of your idea.

You need to start showing people immediately. Don't be shy here. Invite plenty of friends and industry colleagues out for coffee and show them what you have built. Ask them for positive thoughts and constructive feedback. Ask them what they look for when they are buying software.

Critically ask them the kind of questions they would ask potential vendors. Any feedback on the product is good if it is genuine. Make copious notes on the questions they ask you and the ones they would ask in a software demo. Think carefully about detailed answers to each. This can save your bacon when you are demoing the software for real in a room full of potential commercial prospects.

Lastly, ask them if anyone in their network would be interested in seeing it? This is important. The people your network know can often end up being your first clients. Make it clear at this stage that you want to meet them more for market research than sales and their feedback would be invaluable for future development.

No one likes the hard sell, but everyone likes to see nifty new technology that can make their lives easier. Often these invaluable personal recommendations can be where your first business client will emerge from.

From here, you will start to contact these warm introductions through your friends, peers, and industry network. You can have the first introductory meetings with potential clients. Emphasize that these are for research and feedback only. At this stage, you are in exploratory talks with the first potential clients and the aim here is to build a realistic **gap analysis** of what you have in your MVP right now versus what a real client would need to buy and deploy your product.

Your friends are no good anymore. You need to get the MVP in front of real potentially paying customers. Friends will tell you what you have built is great regardless. What you need is cold feedback in the hard light of day. It is better to receive this constructive criticism and feedback right now, than spend any more money enhancing your MVP in the wrong direction, and in a way, that is simply not suitable for your target clients.

Once you have had some initial discussions on the MVP with your first few potential customers, it is time to incorporate this feedback into devising a proper software demo plan, while building out an underlying business development strategy and finding the right team to drive it.

Chapter Summary

- Identify a suitable product developer.
- Apply MoSCoW prioritization to your idea.
- Develop a detailed Product Development Document.
- Manage the development cycle closely.
- Nail down the best version of the MVP possible for your budget.
- Start showing it to friendly folks and think about their feedback.
- Begin contacting warm leads in the industry for more formal demos.
- Build an initial "gap analysis" of product features you are missing based on first demos.

CHAPTER 3

Building a Team

Introduction

It's the team that makes or breaks the business.

Your MVP might be great. The market might need it. The potential could be huge. Investors might be lining up. But if you do not have the team to implement your idea, then the business will go nowhere.

If you read the traditional start-up literature, that is, primarily by people who haven't actually done it but will tell you what they think you should do, you will be told you should hire now for the following roles:

- Business development and marketing
- Finance and accounting
- Manager of operations and operations person
- Human resources
- Operations associate
- Marketing jack-of-all trades
- Salesperson
- Writer
- Product manager/engineers (for tech businesses)
- Computer technician

What a joke. You will not have the money to even pay yourself for at least a year. How are you meant to fund any of these hires?

The CEO, business development and marketing, all operations, product manager, writer, and human resources (ha!) is all you. There is no one else. There won't be for a year or even two. You will have to do virtually every nontechnical role yourself. This will conserve cash but will also eat away at your time and is completely exhausting. The only solution is to focus on the key objectives you want to achieve in each area and go for those. Your time is a precious asset. Use it wisely.

Who to Hire?

Outside of specialist technical areas, recruit for enthusiasm over experience. Skills can be learned. Simple tasks can be picked up quickly. Complex tasks can be learned over time.

In particular, during the first year of operation, hire a couple of smart, enthusiastic young graduates or interns and train them up on the business and the way you want things to run. You can hand over a ton of mindless and manual work to them that will slow you right down (e.g., social media, organizing meetings, emailing prospects, and so on). With the exception of fully technical roles, go for enthusiasm over experience every time.

This is actually fortunate as you simply will not have the cash in the first year to hire full time on a permanent basis, anybody with decent experience in your area. Labor is just too expensive. Yet another reason we located an hour outside Dublin was because the cost of living was much cheaper, and concurrently, so was the cost of staff. In a technology business, once your product is built out, you will spend at least 80 percent of your outgoings on employee wages.

Remember—**Attitude is everything.**

If you get this wrong a couple of times, your lovely little business will be history.

A positive attitude applies to you too as CEO. It is vital to **keep the sunny side up** in the office. By all means, be transparent to your staff on the ups and downs of the business, but stay positive, stay enthusiastic, and keep the team excited about the company's mission and long-term vision. On the down days (and there will be many), try working from home instead. If you can't put on your "Game Face," stay out of the office and come back in when you get your mojo back.

Spend time meeting and speaking to **local universities and higher education institutes in your local area.** Ask them what graduate or placement (i.e., intern) students are available. Universities can be an amazing source for local expertise and quality staff, right in your backyard. Often, they can offer the company access to inhouse specialists and onsite learning resources. I used our regional third level technology institute on many occasions (our first office was based in their incubation center) and most of the graduate hires I made remain in the company to this day. A few of them are heading up the core teams.

This new staff will be a clean, blank slate for you to educate. To successfully bring them up to speed, you are going to have to **conduct a lot of tutorials** and educational sessions exploring all the aspects of the industry, the company, the future strategy, and of course your own technology. Record all these sessions. Try to keep each one to about an hour and focus on the core topics in the industry first, before branching out into related and subtopics. Put together a shared worksheet with about twenty initial subject areas and invite the team to add suggestions and requests to bulk out their understanding.

When I set up the business, I conducted many long sessions covering all aspects of the business and how our organization fit within it. My new employees referred to these recordings constantly. These formed a core part of the future employee induction process. What at the early days was theoretical knowledge became embedded experience as the MVP was finalized and then the marketing and business development process was executed. After a year, they knew the funds industry inside out.

Attend entrepreneur and technology meetups. You will meet people at such events that are interested in joining a start-up and open to new ideas. Some may even share your vision and enthusiasm. They can be a great catalyst to get you started and provide the passion early on to get the first MVP build and ready to deploy.

You will not be able to compete financially with the large established companies in your industry. **Don't even try.** Instead, focus on what you can offer the potential staff. Flexible working conditions, an exciting start-up environment, a shorter commute, decent holidays, and the chance to receive equity in the longer term from the company's Employee Share Options Pool (often called an "ESOP").

In Ireland, there are a huge number of global technology businesses based in Dublin that pay extremely high salaries to their technology and operational staff. We could not hope to match them in the early years. Instead, we located outside the city in a town with lower costs of property and little traffic. Many initial staff had previously spent hours each day trying to reach Dublin city center on poor and unreliable public transport. We were able to offer them a higher quality of life with a lower cost of living. That's pretty attractive. Many could not wait to leave the three- and four-hour round-trip commute to come work for an exciting, fast growing business.

Hiring overseas staff has its own challenges. It is much better if you already know the first couple of international hires prior to launching the business. An existing personal or professional relationship makes the employee onboarding process much smoother. Overseas staff will need to be self-starters, who are able to strongly motivate themselves, especially in the early days. There won't be that much company oversight on the ground.

The first foreign hires you make (besides some outsourced technology development) will most likely be in business development and sales. Look for a strong track record, and in interviews, set your "BS radar" to the max. Make sure you meet the individual in person at least once. By far the best way to find a good, reliable salesperson in a new market is to have someone recommended to you personally by a peer that you trust and respect. Weekly video and catch up calls will make the oversight process easier and enable overseas staff to feel part of the team. Bring them back to base every quarter (if at all possible) and bulk up the sales staff with relationship and client management resources as the business expands.

In your early years, I suggest **avoiding ex-public sector employees or those that have worked for exceptionally large, slow moving organizations**. In my view, they are not suited to the early stage start-up environment. Other people might have different experiences. By all means hire them as advisors or on specific pieces of work that require their technical expertise (e.g., scientific knowledge, new AI algorithms, and so on). I have found that people from this kind of background are **not commercial minded**. It's not their fault. They have never had to be.

Many ex-big company employees expect stuff to be done for them. They are also more risk averse and can be slower to turn decisions into actions. Of course, they will tell you that they are sick of the bureaucracy of big business and want to work in a dynamic start-up culture, but the reality can be a major shock for them.

I have often heard people with this kind of background propose ideas like "we should target Japan" or "let's put out a new marketing flyer." I have had to turn around and say, "Great idea—go home and tell your wife you will be in Japan till next year." They can often get shocked by this. In a start-up, there is simply no one else to do it.

That reality that each team member needs to be **a jack of a trades as well as probably a master of one** can be a big surprise for staff coming from an organization where there is always milk in the fridge and someone to buy the toilet roll. They often don't understand how to live exclusively on their wits and that's what your company will be doing for the first few years.

When you do start to hire successful, experienced staff from big organizations (as you probably will when the business starts to scale), **move slowly.** Get to know the potential employee well personally and professionally. Do this over a number of months. Really try and understand what motivates them and educate them on the reality of working for a fast-growing start-up. Spend multiple coffees telling them about the company's exciting future plans but spend as much time discussing the long hours, level of commitment, and flexibility required from all the staff to make success a reality.

Before the seed round, anyone from a big company with decent experience who doesn't know you personally would probably run a mile at jacking in a "Big 4" role with great benefits, to join your little, unfunded outfit (and if they don't, their better half will do that for them). You are more likely to hire someone like this **after you draw down your seed round**. By then, you will have some cash in the bank and the company will be becoming better known. This will generate interest among staff at the larger companies in your market.

What the **"big company hire"** does is bring credibility to your business and help the company grow up and professionalize. The hire can bring many years of corporate experience and is often exactly what the CEO needs at this point to put proper, scalable processes in place. These hires can work out great if you get them right. My first blue chip hire is now the CEO of the company.

Remember, for you as the CEO and founder, **even one bad apple** thrown into your little pond does not cause a ripple. It will cause a tsunami that can drag you all down.

All the new staff must be placed on a **mandatory six-month probation period.** Feel free to extend this by another six months if you have any reservations **whatsoever** about their performance over that period. Some new staff just need a bit longer to bed into an organization and that's fine. We all learn in different ways and sometimes it pays off to be patient. However, those who do not perform over time will breed resentment among the rest of your team and the impact on the company's morale can be devastating.

Many new businesses go belly-up because the **internal dynamics haven't gelled together** properly, and the team is not united. Don't tolerate staff that are a distraction. You are on a mission and you have no time for passengers or parasites. Everyone has to be aligned and focused relentlessly on reaching your goals.

Ruthlessly purge the team of any politicizing, gossiping, or unacceptable behavior. It is just not worth keeping them. There are a million other companies they can join that feed off internal politics and jockeying for position. Your business cannot afford to be one of them.

How to Behave as a CEO?

Your behavior will be the primary driver of the new culture that evolves in the company.

You, as the CEO, need to be approachable and helpful at all times. This means your door is genuinely open to the staff and they are expected to be able to come to you with every problem under the sun. At least in the first year or two. By the time the company has been seed funded and you have onboarded a successful first client, you can start to push back gently, and gradually delegate more and more responsibility to your key lieutenants.

All this takes time. Both your employees and you have to build confidence in their ability to interface directly with clients, external contractors, key advisors, and even some investors. You will always be needed for more senior decisions, but by having a "we tried our best" and **sincerely**

fostering a "no blame" culture, your team will become more confident in their ability and willingness to manage the day-to-day business decisions.

What you need to do to prepare your team from the get-go is to clearly articulate the key company targets in the year ahead. Bring your whole team up to speed each week with key updates and let them ask questions and encourage feedback.

Each quarter, write down the **five big objectives** for that period on one of those large (and cheap) whiteboards in massive text and place it against the wall in the center of the office. Make sure everyone can see it. Sometimes, during the day-to-day morass, we all need to be reminded by staring at our objectives in the face. It is far too easy to get diverted with tasks that do not add value to the company and its valuation (e.g., sales tax returns, grant applications, funding requests, and so on).

Freely adjust annual and quarterly objectives as time goes by, but keep the team updated and constantly measure progress against the core milestones of product development, client acquisitions, and revenue generation. That is what you will need to reach to secure the next funding round.

By examining every opportunity and cost in the context of the company's core objectives, the team can see through the "noise" of day-to-day start-ups chaos and remain aligned on delivering your strategic objectives.

By **Series A** funding time, you as the CEO should be used as a point of escalation for clients and serious internal issues. That is, the company can run day-to-day without much involvement from you. The core team, that has probably been with you from the early days, will be experienced and trained enough to handle the day-to-day business and resolve low level issues, as well as manage the product development, marketing, sales cycle, and technology functions.

This means, you as the CEO should then have more time to focus on:

- Defining the business strategy
- Working on fundraising
- Touching base with clients and their management team every month
- Be wheeled in at the final phase of business development to "bless" a new client contract

How to Behave Toward Your Staff?

Insist that your staff takes their **holidays**. This is crucial if you don't want them to be completely burned out and become overwhelmed by the work rate. Tell them that not taking vacation is not a sign of company commitment, it is a sign that they can't keep on top of their workload.

Some working cultures (e.g., the United States) can be slow to come around this way of thinking, but if you don't, you have no hope of keeping seasoned, experienced employees on board as the company grows. This is for the quite simple reason that experienced staff (being older) will have families and children and partners that share their life. We had to sit down the U.S. employees and tell them that they were expected to take five weeks' holiday. It was a big cultural change, but it meant they were much happier and motivated in the long term. They were also a lot less likely to leave in the long run.

If possible, try and have everyone (including yourself) take **a week off every quarter**. Having a decent break every three months helps keep the staff motivated. It won't always be possible in the early years but should be manageable by Series A time.

If you have a **cofounder** (maybe a great developer), that's great. They will be a huge help as the business expands and they will act as a sounding board to move strategy and ideas forward. You can discuss together the kind of culture you wish to foster at the company and the HR policies you will put in place.

But make no mistake here—**you** are the boss. One person needs to be the CEO and the ultimate decision maker. It won't work otherwise. Disagreements will end in arguments. Arguments will end in rancor and that will poison your business.

Also, VCs will expect there to be someone in charge. Remember what the United States said about not knowing who to call when they wanted to speak to "Europe"? Don't fall into that trap. There can be informed debate and collaborative discussion, but you are the final decision maker. There is no other way it can work. It's a recipe for chaos—not structured expansion.

One Silicon Valley VC told me that he wanted one single person in charge, so he knew whose throat to put his hands around if things went south. That's the reality.

So, you are the boss, but you will need help. In these early days, there is a bunch of painful operation and marketing stuff that has to be done and is essential to start growing. You can easily train a **college intern or placement student** to help with this.

Managing the Team Day-to-Day

The following are some **quick tips to keep in mind** when you are building the new team:

- Be nice and polite to everyone. This should go without saying but is easier said than done on a down day.
- Let them know you all are on an exciting, game changing mission together. Let them feel the excitement when you work together.
- Have them involved in everything and all aspects of the business.
- By giving new staff invaluable experience, they won't want to leave.
- Have **everyone** at the company involved in the sales cycle, especially in the early years.
- Tell your staff the truth, but stay positive too.
- Clearly communicate the key objectives each quarter and over the year ahead.
- Praise staff generously when they meet their targets and excessively when they exceed them.
- Give small bonuses whenever you can and be flexible about personal matters like childcare, medical emergencies, and so on. Staff remember your response to these matters for a long time.
- If you win a big contract, give everyone a pay rise. Make it clear that when the company prospers, so will the team.
- Insist on everyone taking their holidays and you should too. They will follow your example.
- Actively communicate that you are looking forward to allocating the Employee Share Pool to the new team in due course and they will receive it over three years (sometimes called having shares "vested").

- Demonstrate to them that their good ideas can come to real fruition at the company (e.g., setting up a social media group or designing a new product feature). This can be a huge vote of recognition and confidence for a young professional starting their career. They will love you forever for the validation.
- Illustrate repeatedly to your team that the best idea **always** carries the day. If their idea on something is better than yours, then their idea is what you execute.
- As the team grows, spend time cultivating and **building a core management team**. These three or four department heads will run the business for you day-to-day. This allows you to work **on** the business and **not in** the business. If the time comes that you wish to move on, one of these experienced staff will be able to move up into the CEO role.

If you are not a "people" person, **then give up now**. Or at the very least, find a people person cofounder to be the CEO. Someone who lives for social and personal contact.

You have to love your staff and do everything in your power to empower them—financially, personally, and often emotionally. It is a rollercoaster. You are going to be spending a lot of time with these people (much more than your own family), so choose them carefully.

Ask yourself, could you imagine travelling with this person for twenty-four hours on economy class and then staying at a budget hotel for weeks while you work closely together fourteen hours a day?

And lastly, **remember the "Golden Rule."** There are many, many things in this business that will be outside of your control. One thing that is definitely within your control is how you relate to people. Don't be obnoxious. If you are, you will have no loyalty or commitment from the team. You may think you have troops behind you but when the fighting starts, they will not follow you into battle.

Chapter Summary

- Hire for attitude, not experience.
- Take on at least one intern to help with social media and mundane tasks.
- Universities are a great resource for staff, as are Meetup groups and other entrepreneurs.
- Avoid ex-public servants/large company employees before you are seed funded.
- The behavior of the CEO sets the culture for every new organization.
- Encourage staff to take holidays.
- Give autonomy freely and choose the best idea (not necessarily yours).
- Encourage an atmosphere of feedback and open discussion.
- Be transparent but upbeat.
- Never be obnoxious. Tomorrow will be better.

CHAPTER 4

Managing Company Cash Flow

Introduction to "the Struggle"

Some experienced entrepreneurs would say this is the most important chapter in the book. It's true in that if you don't become a **master at cash flow management,** then it's all over, and quickly.

Ask yourself this question about your personal life. Do you lie awake in bed at night worrying about money?

If you do, that's great. If you don't, then give up now. You simply won't make it.

This critical question needs to be asked by you and **honestly** answered **before** you take the decision to become an entrepreneur

Perhaps you have a cofounder. Maybe they are the businessperson and you are the techie. That's great— let them worry. But someone has to. Let me state this twice—**someone** has to. 24/7 for those first couple of years.

You will keep hearing that 90 percent of new businesses fail within the first couple of years. And why do they fail? Because they run out of cash. Remember, that is **not** going to be you.

Welcome to what experienced entrepreneurs call as "The **Struggle**."

It's aptly named because a giant, herculean struggle of stress and resilience is exactly what it is.

Setting up and scaling a technology business is a **supreme balancing act.** In fact, the art of growing a successful start-up business is a constant crisis management.

You are always about to run out of money. **Always**. If this fills you with horror, please keep your day job and your cash, and put it into a savings account.

Personal Finances in Year 1

You are an experienced expert in your field. You should have some savings, and if not, then in the year before you start the business, start saving hard. You will need $20,000 to $30,000 for your MVP and another $20,000 for business expenses to get through year one. You also need money saved or income available for personal living expenses. I wish this weren't the case, but I am afraid there is no magic money tree in the real world.

You may have to consider **refinancing your house**. If you don't own a property, perhaps take out an unsecured **personal loan** to develop your MVP. This personal loan should be enough to pay the MVP costs but also the loan payments for Year 1. That is, if you need $25,000 to get your MVP developed, then borrow $30,000. The additional $5,000 can stay in your bank account and should be used to meet the first year (or even two) of loan repayments.

In addition, in the year before you start the company, **save another $20,000 for working capital.** If you have been working in your industry for a decade and have a good job, saving an amount like this should be manageable. No one said it would be easy. Nothing about building this business will be easy.

The **ideal solution** is to have a partner/spouse who has an income that will cover household necessities for Year 1. That should include mortgage payments, childcare, household bills, and so on. It can't be overstated how less stressful Year 1 will be if you do not have to worry about putting food on the table or a roof over your children's head.

Consider taking a **short break from your mortgage.** Many banks offer a three-month payment holiday once or twice over the course of a mortgage. It is normally quite easy to arrange and it will give you some breathing space in that first quarter, while you are having the MVP built.

If at all possible, also try and separately **save three months'** realistic and generous personal, living expenses and put them into a separate bank account. Tell your partner, or yourself, that if you ever have to touch this three-month emergency fund, then you will start updating your CV and looking for another job. If you are an expert in your niche, then it will likely take a month to find some work and you will be paid by month three, before your savings run out. This financial cushion will enable you to sleep a bit easier at night.

Lastly, before you leave your current job, ask your bank for a **generous personal overdraft**. I had a $10,000 overdraft for years. I rarely, if ever, used it. But on a couple of occasions in the early years it saved the company's bacon, when a client paid late, taxes were due, or we had a payroll deadline looming.

Managing Company Cash Flow in Year 1

In Year 1, cut back your personal and business costs to the **absolute minimum**. Use the same **MoSCoW Prioritization** methodology you used on your MVP and apply it to both your personal life and new business expenses. What are the essentials of each, versus the nice to have? Adjust your expenses ruthlessly and accordingly. Most new businesses fail because of cash flow. If you don't look after yours like a new-born baby, then your business is toast.

Year 1 will be the toughest year for the company. You have probably never run a business before. You have likely never run a technology business. You have no revenue and you are relying on savings. You have to make that stretch for at least a year and probably into Year 2. No one will give you angel funding until you have a product. No one will give you seed funding until you have a client. Surviving sounds daunting but it can be done—**if** you manage the cash flow carefully.

Have a monthly "**Cash Projection Sheet**" for the rest of the year (at least six months ahead), and within that, have **week by week** columns for the next two months. This is a line by line detail of what you will spend, when you will spend it, and any revenue you expect to receive. Add copious notes, reminders, and alerts to where you may have a weak link in your cashflow chain.

A **detailed and realistic budget** is also invaluable when starting to look for investor funding. VCs and angels see such atrocious financing plans and budgets, that anything half reasonable and realistic will be an improvement on most start-up businesses. The more details you include, the more prudent you appear and the more conscientious you look, having considered all financial angles and likely cashflow outcomes.

In a technology company, more than 80 percent of the post launch spending (after your MVP is built) will likely come from paying employee **salaries**. In your first year, this might be close to zero—unless you have the savings in place pre-revenue to pay someone. It is highly unlikely that the company will be able to pay you a salary until Year 2 at the earliest.

You need to organize and manage tightly both your own personal finances and the company's cash flow for the **first 18 months**. After that time, hopefully, you will have made enough progress to draw down some angel funding. This is often funding from a wealthy individual or an ex-entrepreneur.

In Year 1 of business, once the MVP is paid for, the core company expenses will likely look like this:

- **Wages**—80 percent
- **Rent**—5 percent
- **Server storage**—5 percent
- **Software licenses**—5 percent
- **Miscellaneous costs**—5 percent

A **start-up space** can be useful, as it bundles utility costs together, so you have one monthly fee covering electricity, Internet, heating, and even cleaning. Sometimes this fee will also include access to a meeting space for demos to prospects and potential clients.

Server storage costs will climb as the business grows but should be fairly small in Year 1 of the company. **License fees** will include the monthly software costs of your e-mail, website, possible security certificates, and a simple Customer Relationship Management (CRM) solution.

Miscellaneous costs could include travel to meet a prospective client, lunch and perhaps a (rare) overnight budget hotel, start-ups insurance, and so on.

The typical monthly costs for a new technology business in Year 1 could look like this:

- Wages—$4,000—to pay essential technology development and an intern
- Rent—$400—start-up space
- Server Storage—$200—for example, AWS
- Licenses—$150—for example, GSuite, One Page CRM, Web Hosting, and so on

- Miscellaneous costs—$250—occasional bus tickets, an odd business lunch, a rare flight

That's approximately $5,000 a month or $60,000 over the course of the first year.

You will be unlikely to have all this cash saved (potentially $90,000 in total, including the cost of your MVP).

If you do, great. If you don't, you will have to start using your personal overdraft and credit cards as the money runs out.

Reducing Year 1 costs can be done by working out of a **room at your home** and not paying any wages at all. However, working from home won't cut it, when your prospective new business client wants to come over to your office and check out that you are a real company. Even if you do not have any salaried employees, you will still have to pay some technical maintenance and probably development costs. Also, if you choose not to hire an intern in Year 1, you will be overwhelmed in drudgery once the business starts to gain traction.

You should ask for a **limit increase on your credit cards** before you leave your old job. It's an insurance policy so you can pay urgent bills, that can't be delayed any longer. No one likes doing this, but sometimes it is unavoidable.

As you come to the end of Year 1, you will be heavily engaged in marketing the product and getting that first business client over the line. You will have gathered some traction and market recognition. You do not want the plane to crash at the end of the runway, when it's about to take off.

A good start-up CEO will look at **every available source of funding**—from family and friends, to invoice financing and client license prepayments, to credit card increases, and extended bank loans. Anything to keep the train on the tracks.

Surviving this crazy launch period will **of itself give your company credibility**. After a couple of years, you will be a known and respected vendor in your space and your funding challenges will be strategic, rather than existential. You just have to stay alive long enough to reach that point.

Remember—the number one objective of business is **to stay in business**.

Managing Company Cash Flow in Year 2

As the business scales into Year 2, additional costs can come from business travel (lots of demos and meetings with prospective clients) and the attendance of business events (to get the company name out there), as well as chiefly, the first proper employee hires.

Ideally, some **angel funding** (in excess of $50,000+) going into Year 2 will help meet these new costs and also the expense of some initial hiring. It will be a very welcome bit of breathing space for you.

As the CEO, you have to plan carefully **what meetings are worth travelling for** and what business events (conferences, trade shows, etc.) are worth attending. Every big city has dozens of these. Many won't have the potential buyer for your solution. Some may have too many vendors and not enough prospects. Wrangle the attendee list well in advance and choose which business events to attend carefully.

Conferences, in particular, can be extremely expensive. Every industry has one or two key events annually and you should budget for attending them. Start-up focused events are fine too in the early days, for some exposure, but they are highly unlikely to result in much business or that all important first proper paying business client.

Once you start to employ staff, you will have to start dealing with the **tax authorities** much more regularly than before. There will likely be a six-month gap between when you start paying some proper salaries to the staff and having the money to retain an accountant to manage the company payroll. The onus is **on you** to ensure that these filings and payments are made accurately and on schedule. **Do not** under any circumstances screw up the company taxes. You already have more than enough to keep you awake at night, without adding the taxman to your long list.

How I Managed Company Cash Flow

Managing cash flow is the area that can be the toughest in the early years, and **as the CEO, you are on your own**.

There is no way to sugar-coat this. Advisers can advise and investors can provide funding, but the worry and constant stress of the company cash flow is yours and yours alone.

If you are prone to appearing stressed, do your cash projection and calculations when no-one else is around. Preferably in the **morning** before the staff arrives. That way, you are not taking the stress home with you at the end of the day.

You must learn to **smile through the stress,** both to your team and to yourself; even when you are dying inside because you know the company coffers are empty and payday is coming.

Building detailed financial projections for all the potential company scenarios (**optimistic, pessimistic, and likely**) should be your "resting" mode. It will help clear your mind and bring a sense of calmness and equilibrium to the madness.

How I managed the cashflow stress was by utilizing my long experience in **project management**. This helped to bring some structure to the businesses financial and operational chaos. It was the only way I knew how to organize the company; especially in the early days when you are simultaneously acting as the CEO, the marketing and sales department, the product manager, and the whole accounting team!

I **watched the bottom line relentlessly**; trying to think of any way to reduce costs and get a good deal. I negotiated free banking fees for the first year. I drafted and filed the company accounts myself (and made a mess of them!). I used legal contracts and business templates that I bought cheaply online for the first client. Anything at all to try and pare back the company's outgoings and extend our runway.

On three or four occasions, I did some additional unrelated consulting work, concurrently, while trying to grow my tech company. All that money went into the business. I had to do this, not just in Ireland but at multiple locations worldwide. I was gone for weeks on end trying to manage both businesses. This took my focus off the technology company somewhat and slowed down our growth and development, but I had no choice. I needed the funds to keep both the company solvent and a roof over the head of my young family.

A year into the business I was personally out of cash. I took a second personal loan from the bank to live on. Then I borrowed a small amount of money from my family and applied for grant funding from the excellent Irish government start-up agency, Enterprise Ireland. They placed me on a program specifically for new entrepreneurs. This program was called New Frontiers and it paid me $18,000 as a personal bursary over six months.

I also applied for copious amounts of **grant funding and low-cost loans** from the Local Enterprise Boards. Some of it was approved and some of it was refused. All funds received made a big difference to cash flow in those early years. This included cofunding contributions to attend trade shows and conferences, as well as some assistance with paying our first employee salaries.

I worked from home in Year 1. This saved on office rent for a year but once the business started to get some traction and with a young family at home, I had to have a dedicated office space to focus on the company. We found a great space very cheap at the **Business Incubation Centre** of our local university.

I didn't get to pay myself a salary in any form until we had our seed funding round in place. At that point, I was earning a quarter of the salary I had made in London three years earlier.

To try and raise some more funding, I entered **start-up competitions**. This was sometimes a distraction, but we needed the money and the media exposure was good for the business. We won Europe's largest start-up competition, which gave us a no-strings attached cash prize of $60,000.

We received that money literally days before the company was due to go bankrupt. We had just lost a big deal in London due to the Brexit vote. No one wanted to buy our compliance software, when they did not know what the future compliance rules were going to be. The prize money gave us another six months' runway and I was able to secure our seed round just as that cash ran out.

I had three years in which the company was only ever a week or less away from going under. It was living in a constant state of impending financial collapse. At every point, we managed to pull through; to keep going that bit longer. I learned to become very resilient, but it was extremely tough and could have extracted a steep toll on my mental health.

You are so far into the process, **there is no going back**. You will do absolutely everything to survive and leave no stone unturned. I worked part time on other consulting projects just to try and keep the company alive. It worked but it slowed everything down. It was also an extremely stressful juggling act.

As the money ran out, I pulled in many friends with the specific experience I required. From video production and user design to digital marketing and social media. All of this helped and enabled the business to keep growing. It also kept a lid on our expenses as we got some traction.

By that point, I was well into Year 2. There was no money left to pay anyone anyway, but we were just about to have onboard our first decent sized paying client. $50,000 in angel funding saved the company from going under.

You never have enough saved up. Revenue always takes longer than you think to generate and there are always unanticipated expenses that can wreck your cash flow. You need to focus nonstop on what they are and on making sure you get your hands on the cash to overcome them.

All those esteemed business gurus who talk about "paying yourself first" have never run a new fast-growing technology business. It is just not possible when you are trying to get off the ground and stretch your meager savings as far as they can possibly go.

As I grew the company, we decided to **hire extensively from the local university**. It was situated next door to our office and had a number of great courses, including a combined business and technology degree. Students came to us with a basic knowledge of coding and some exposure to business.

We recruited numerous work placement students as part of that degree program and then took them on gradually after graduation as full-time hires. This "try before you buy" approach worked really well. It gave me the opportunity to train these graduates in our industry from scratch. It also kept the cash flow impact to a minimum, until we had the funding to pay them properly as employees.

Young people are incredibly conscientious these days. Many grew up in the post-2008 crash. They value working in a team, striving together for a worthwhile, bigger purpose, and appreciate the autonomy and responsibility they receive quickly when working in a small start-up.

Conclusion

As the long start-up phase grinds out over Year 1 and you start to run down your savings, you can expect to have to hit your personal credit card and overdraft hard. When it came to finalize our seed funding round, on top of the two personal loans I had already spent, I had over $40,000 of company expenses on my personal credit cards.

I see no easy way around this. Unless you are lucky enough to secure an angel investor incredibly early in the scaling process.

If the prospect of accruing massive personal, business-related debt does not appeal to you, then you are better off sticking to your day job.

Chapter Summary

- The year before company set up, start saving hard. Aim for at least $30,000.
- Borrow the rest. Take out a personal loan to cover the MVP build and one year of loan payments.
- Consider refinancing your home and/or taking a mortgage break.
- Put three months' emergency savings in a bank account and if you have to touch it, start looking for a job.
- A partner that will cover Year 1 household essentials, while you get the company set up is worth their weight in gold.
- Master cashflow projections and update your Cash Projection Sheet constantly.
- Try to avoid paying any salaries in Year 1.
- Consider low cost company loans or government start-up funding.
- Apply for start-up competitions to win funding and raise awareness and investor interest.
- Watch the bottom line relentlessly.
- Be prepared to hit personal credit cards hard in the lead up to finalizing your seed funding round.

CHAPTER 5

Marketing the Business

Introduction

Marketing your business and product should be at the forefront of the company strategy **from Day 1**. Before the MVP is finished. Before you have written a Business Plan. Before you have even had coffee with a potential client.

In selling Business to Business (B2B) software, **the market is much smaller.** You can focus and target marketing in a way that is harder to do, when you are trying to crack the huge retail market. On the other hand, one of the biggest challenges you will face is the **exceedingly long procurement cycle of most huge global businesses**.

As you get setup and have your technology partners working on the first version of the product, you need to start the process of letting the world know you exist. It does not matter how great your technology is or how ground-breaking your innovation, if no one knows you exist, you will go nowhere.

In the early days, you focused on building a brand, spreading the word, and getting the company's name out there. The really fantastic news is that you can do this very cheaply nowadays and often even completely free. The age of social media has allowed small companies to compete nearly evenly, with large global businesses.

A clever, **consistent** multipronged marketing campaign can bring your business to the notice of many of the companies in the sector that you are targeting. Done consistently, over time it will give the company credibility, provide the groundwork for your business development strategy, and if done correctly, enable you to market directly to a captive audience that is interested in your solution.

Implementing Your Marketing Strategy

In the first year of business, the company needs to focus on building some initial recognition in the business niche that will be your future marketplace.

As soon as the company e-mail account is set up, add a **Signature** at the bottom. Not just the usual "CEO Company XYZ." Below that, add a tagline for the business. For example, *"Providing the fastest data connections to the healthcare business."* This should be a slogan that can be put on all marketing and publicity material. Keep it short and keep it snappy. It can be updated and refined as you go along but do make sure it encapsulates the **core value proposition** of your business in one sentence.

Also, feel free to put a **link to the company deck** you have created or even **embed** the document if you wish. If you win any prizes, receive an award, or even if you are shortlisted for one, place a line below your title that announces this great news (e.g., *"Shortlisted for New York's best MedTech Start-ups"*). Every e-mail and every reply that comes out of your company should have a signature like this, which acts as an ongoing, passive form of marketing to your audience.

Set up all core social media channels now. Twitter, Facebook, Instagram (if it makes business sense), and especially LinkedIn. You will be spending a lot of time on LinkedIn over the next few months, so try and become an expert user as soon as you can. Share the new business accounts across your personal social media network (e.g., on your Facebook page) and ask your friends to follow/like the company and also to **share on their pages too**. This should get you at least a couple of hundred followers immediately.

Social Media takes time. There is no doubt about it and no way around it. It pays great dividends if done well and consistently over your first year, and the best thing about it is that it's basically free. However, content needs to be valuable, interesting, and consistent. It all involves a huge amount of sharing, commenting, posting, and liking.

It is so much easier to build a great, ongoing social media strategy, if you **personally already have a good online presence** and are recognized as a thought leader in your space. When I set up my company, I already had over twelve thousand LinkedIn connections. I was a member of dozens of relevant LinkedIn start-ups and financial technology ("FinTech") groups and had written and published books and articles in that area, while also commenting many times on all the social media. Building a new social media profile for the company was not that difficult and the business soon had four times as many Twitter followers as me.

Even if you are not a recognized thought leader in your niche, it does not matter. What you need is **six months of regular, interesting, and informed posts shared every day**. Even if it's just someone else's content with your commentary, that is fine too. You can spend five minutes every day sharing that in the early stages, as you get your MVP dusted off.

After six months, it will be obvious to the industry that you are not just a "fly by night" operator and you are the real deal. You know and care about what's going on in your space and you are building a great solution to address its pain points. After funding, **credibility** is often the number one problem for start-up technology companies. A sustained social media and marketing campaign can help close that gap. Two years into the business, you will have larger prospects contacting you out of the blue looking for product demos. Junior staff at leading VCs will be e-mailing you to talk about your progress and kick the tires.

The very first job you should give that first placement student or intern is the **management of the company's social media campaign**. I also recommend this intern is the first person you hire in the company. They are cheap, enthusiastic, looking for great experience, and normally technologically savvy. In the interview, before you hire them, ask them **in detail** for an honest assessment of their proficiency of each platform. You devise the strategy, but you want them to implement it. They will love the autonomy.

Set up a simple "**Social Media Calendar Spreadsheet**" and hand over ownership of it to them. This calendar should contain all the social media postings that will be made over the next week or two and some that are planned longer term. This could include blog posts, sharing others' interesting content, posting a short company video, and making a marketing announcement.

Aim to have at least one new blog post a week, one new short video every two weeks (ideally if you are discussing some new industry trend or a company development), one or two daily interesting posts in the market, and one marketing notification each week (in the early days, it can simply be "Follow us on social media at XYZ" or "Make sure to check our website and sign up to our newsletter," etc.). You can post the company's blog posts and marketing twice but it's best to leave a week in between each time. No one wants to be bored by repetitive content.

Once you have set up a **company page on LinkedIn**, then **set up your own LinkedIn group**, for example, "Key Trends in XYZ industry." This group will cover new trends in the industry and will be hosted and managed by you. You can also add "Powered by Company ABC" after the name if you like. Share it to your personal LinkedIn profile and encourage everyone you know in your industry to join it. You should be able to achieve a few hundred members within a week.

This **captive audience** of your industry can be especially useful to you as a walled garden form of soft marketing. Everyday post in there at least one or two interesting pieces of news from your industry. Set up a Google alert on the topic you want, and the news will be e-mailed directly to your inbox every day. Try and add a comment with every news item you post. It can be as simple as "great article" or "interesting read," but it is much more powerful if you have a considered sentence. For example, "This is not a bad piece, but it misses out on the new healthcare technology rules in California." It should be something of value that demonstrates and reiterates day after day, both you and the company's expertise and knowledge of your niche.

Reshare the group regularly on your personal and company LinkedIn page, and over time, it can become the go-to group on LinkedIn for your particular area. Invite all companies you meet to join, their senior staff, and any potential investors you are speaking to. They will be impressed.

The key tenet with your group is that it is for **thought leadership and not business development.** However, all interesting points related to the company (e.g., sharing a conference and saying "we can't wait to attend this exciting event") and any new company commentary can be posted here, including all blog posts and company marketing from time to time.

These groups even allow you to make a weekly "**Announcement**" that is sent directly to all the members' LinkedIn messages and appears as a notification when they log in. Use these announcements strategically and carefully, to update the group of key developments in the industry and also interesting updates about the company. It is a great way to funnel news directly to potential prospects.

Set up a **Meetup** group in your area (or the closest big city) that focuses on key trends in your industry (also "Powered by company ABC"). Share this across social media regularly and in time, as you add members, you will be able to organize a relaxed business event when you are ready to launch the product. You will be able to find a few interesting participants from your LinkedIn group that can sit on the panel alongside you and discuss all the exciting news from the industry, as well as the launch of your new solution.

Plug your website into **Google Analytics** so you can keep an eye on the web traffic and how people are spending time on your site. Then set up a **blog page** on the site and once **every week write five short paragraphs** covering what's going on of interest in the industry and also with your company. This is not as difficult as it sounds. Pick one or two of the main developments that week in your area and give your view on it. Mention the latest update from the company (e.g., "very excited as the new product is getting finalized") and share this across all your social media channels.

Once you have **four blog posts published,** sign up to a free **newsletter software** generator and announce that you are launching a company newsletter. This **monthly** newsletter will consist of all the blog posts you make; plus, one or two interesting developments in the market, as well as any key update from the company. Nowadays, these sort of newsletters are nearly generated automatically, and they can be scheduled for a specific date and time. This is what professional companies do. It is not that difficult, and it gives you lots of credibility.

A few months after starting out, **contact a local newspaper** and tell them who you are and what you are doing. Tell them you hope to generate substantial employment in the local area, and you are really hoping the company will put your town on the map, as a hotspot for new technology innovation. Ask them to run a small piece about you (if they don't already offer) and share this repeatedly across social media (at regular intervals). Now you've been featured in the press and you can add that to your company deck.

E-mail a few of the **industry news websites** in your market and ask them if you can write an article for them. Emphasize that this is **not** a marketing or business development piece but will be a thought leadership article, filled with interesting analysis and insight for their readers. Revisit your recent blog posts and spend an hour or two restructuring them, to make up a decent seven-hundred-word piece on the new trends and key developments in your space.

This article should be neutrally toned and indirectly emphasize your experience (e.g., *"Over my twenty years in FinTech, I have never seen such a complicated regulatory landscape as right now."*), while mentioning all the exciting new technology solutions that will benefit the industry in the near future.

Ensure the article includes your **name, job title, e-mail address, and website** below, as well as a one liner telling the reader who you are. For example, *"Shane Brett is the CEO of Global Technologies, a new Irish FinTech company revolutionizing the investment industry."* When this is published, share it far and wide (especially with potential clients and investors), even place a link to it in your e-mail signature and on your website. If you do a good job, you will be asked back, and a monthly or bimonthly article like this can be a massive piece of credibility marketing to the business. At every business coffee, investor meeting, or prospect, demo you conduct, ensure you ask them if they have read your article, and if not, then send it to them or have a printed version ready to leave behind.

Make a number of fairly **regular short videos** discussing the new developments in the industry and your company. With modern technology, this can be done semiprofessionally and quickly for free. Filming these videos with your intern is a great way to get used to pitching to investors and clients. Playback the videos many times. Notice your mistakes. How your voice sounds and if you speak too slow or fast. After a few videos, it will get easier and you will have a good insight into how you appear when you present the business to an investor.

Lastly, **Podcasts** have a great place in social media and marketing your business. You may not have time to do one in the early days, but over time, have your intern interview you over the course of an hour and publish it everywhere. Podcasts give you a real chance to demonstrate the breadth of your knowledge in the industry and your passion for advancing it.

Keep most of the questions to the industry, and then toward the end, you can have a question on the latest developments at the company.

As the company grows, it may also be worthwhile joining a more formal **industry trade group** in your sector. These can be expensive, but they are under pressure to offer "Start-up" rates for small businesses and increasingly many do. I joined an exciting and well regarded, brand new trade group for a few hundred dollars a year. We were encouraged to advertise ourselves as "Founding Members" and were tagged in their social media posts, as well as invited to many important events, conferences, and trade fairs.

A final interesting source of free and valuable marketing is applying for and joining "**Accelerator**" programs in your industry. These programs tend to be run over a number of weeks and months, and are often sponsored by a large global company. It is a way for these big institutions to keep up to date with what is happening on the ground and at the forefront of innovation. Many will offer a sum of cash (typically $30,000 to $100,000) in return for a small equity stake in the business. They will promise support, mentoring, and assistance with refining your investment pitch, while offering partnership opportunities to the winner. While solid business opportunities do not often bear fruit, they can be a source of considerable positive publicity if you make it onto the program and are often tracked and followed by VC investors.

It can also be a place to begin a relationship with a potential VC and meet other start-ups looking at the same market. The time commitment may be considerable, so it is important that they add value to your business and do not divert the company from getting the product finalized and in front of its first potential customers.

Conclusion

All of these marketing channels, working together over time, offer a largely free way for a small new business like yours to build a solid following and generate industry credibility.

Remember, in the early years, **everyone in the company is in marketing and sales.** This can be difficult for more experienced hires to understand. What it means is that it is up to everyone on the team, regardless of their formal role, to advance awareness of the company to the wider world. It needs to be every team member's responsibility. Not just yours.

Good marketing increases the value of the business. Company brand is often the great intangible asset on the balance sheet, and in the early days, yours will not be worth much. However, it will increase in value as you onboard a few good clients and build the business, market awareness, and enhance company credibility.

Chapter Summary

- Build a marketing strategy and hand over implementation to an intern.
- Construct a Social Media Spreadsheet Calendar that the intern can execute, and you can oversight.
- Social media should be your focus. Its free and highly effective if quality content is consistently posted over at least six months.
- Set up company e-mail signatures and embed the company deck in all the e-mails.
- Contact local newspapers to run a news story about you.
- Post a regular blog piece.
- After 4 articles, set up a company newsletter.
- Contact industry websites and ask them if you can write a thought leadership piece on future trends in your industry.
- Complete regular short videos capturing your thoughts on the latest news from the industry and how your company can help.
- Record a regular short podcast on your niche and publish it on social media.

PART II

CHAPTER 6

Pricing the Product

Introduction

There have been whole books written on pricing software. And rightly so. It is a complex and difficult area to get right.

Software is unlike nearly every other business. All the cost on making the product is incurred upfront. That's often 90 percent of the required kick-off capital to get out of the gate. Once the product is built, it is built.

Of course, the software needs to be maintained and updated where appropriate (likely every quarter), but once the core product exists, **it can be resold and resold and resold** with little development cost. That is the reason VCs love to invest in technology companies; **especially** when you have already built the product and you need money to scale it. It is a **"build once and sell many times model."** The potential profitability is huge.

Once your product exists and is road tested, the additional variable costs primarily relate to finding, implementing, and managing new clients and particularly hiring the right team to execute the scaling strategy. A good start-up CEO can carefully match off the funding coming in to resource the business, with the revenue expected from new client deals.

Nailing down the pricing of the software correctly takes time. Accept that this is an evolving process. One that will change as your client base changes and moves from smaller mid-tier players in the industry, to the big global companies spread all around the world.

Potential Pricing Models

When considering the best pricing model for the software, consider the following popular options:

1. **Per user**—The most common and easy to understand. A core license fee for each user of the solution. This fee may be reduced as the number of users increase (e.g., 20 percent discount per user, after the first 100 users deploy). Many large organizations will expect a per user discount as they roll out the software to more and more teams.

2. **Per client**—A fixed fee for that organization. Larger companies may demand this fee model but resist if at all possible. The model offers little upside revenue growth. At the very least, limit the contract to one year with a pricing model review thereafter.

3. **Per location**—The clients' Singapore office pays a flat fee for unlimited use. The New York offices pay a separate fee (the same or negotiated separately) for unlimited use. You will likely need some version of this "Per Location" model in place, as you target the large global behemoths.

4. **Per team**—An initial team as the client pays for unlimited use across their team (and/or for their specific use case). Then when the organization wishes to roll it out to other teams, they pay a similar (or slightly reduced fee) for the new team to onboard. This can be a good way to establish an initial footprint in a large organization, with plenty of potential upside.

5. **Revenue share**—Have your client upsell the solution to their client base. Then split the revenue between you. This can sometimes be possible if your client's client would have use for the solution or can be charged for reporting or data coming out of the system. That kind of shared revenue model can be attractive in the early days, as your client is actively promoting your solution to their customer base. This model increases your credibility in the industry and raises recognition and market awareness. These are all key drivers of your valuation.

6. **A mix of the above**—A minimum monthly flat fee with a variable upside as more users come onto your platform. **This is the preferred pricing model** if you can get your clients to agree.

For example, many B2B start-ups would often insist on a minimum $5,000 per month flat fee. That is low enough not to frighten potential clients or their procurement team. It probably equates roughly to the cost of 1 skilled full-time employee (often referred to as an "FTE").

That $5,000 flat fee per month might cover (say) an initial 30 users. The client might have 20 users on implementation, so that gave them some good upside user growth, at no additional cost to them. That can be highly attractive and make you look like a good potential software partner. Each user after 30 and below (say) 100 could then be charged $100 per month. Over 100 users that could be discounted to (say) $75 per month. A model like this makes sense for you economically and is easier to get past a client's procurement department as it looks like they are getting a good deal.

Clients will promise they will roll out the solution to other teams and different offices. Sometimes that will happen. Sometimes it won't. To protect yourself, you need a **decent minimum charge per client with a variable upside as they onboard more users**.

When I started my technology company, pricing the software was the **single hardest area** to get right in those early years. Probably because I knew little about software and how to price it. We knew there was a market for the solution, we knew it would solve clients' pain, but we hadn't nailed down what price the market would bear. As a brand-new company, it is extremely hard to ask prospective clients what they should pay and receive an objective answer.

We decided to work backwards instead. Pre our seed funding, we were not focused on "Break Even" or profitability. We were focused on getting some clients over the line. That way, we could use them as references to raise more money from investors. Profitable revenue streams could—and should—wait till post the Series A fund raise.

We knew for a Series A round, the company would need at least $1 million in "run-rate" revenue (i.e., revenue contracted in the year ahead) and a healthy sale pipeline to convert. We also knew, for a seed funding round (outside Silicon Valley), we would need to demonstrate some tangible initial traction; a respected first client, with some scaling revenue (i.e., increasing over time) coming in the door.

This meant, we needed to land a good, well respected reference client. What we charged for that client on Day 1 wasn't that important. It was more important to have some revenue coming in and to demonstrate to the investors that there would be some great revenue growth over the next year or two, as they bedded in our solution and rolled it out to other teams and locations.

Pricing for Your Seed Funding Round

When you are working out how much to charge clients, the golden rule from Day 1 is to **keep raising the price until you meet solid market resistance.**

You will know when that happens because the only thing that stops a deal from going forward is your pricing "Rate Card" (this is your standard pricing sheet for the solution and associated services). Once that becomes the key resistance point for clients, then you need to take a downward look at your pricing and adjust it accordingly.

It's fine to mark down the fees you will charge in year one. Put in the contract an "upward only" pricing review in year two. This gives you a chance to capture lost initial revenue and the impact of the year one price reduction on revenue can be neutralized and "bought back" by higher pricing in subsequent years.

What is important is having the contract in place. Just because your client is paying $2,000 a month on Day 1, certainly doesn't mean they can't be paying $12,000 a month in year three. Once your product adds value and the client learns to trust you and the technology, the barriers to substantial upward price movement are much smaller.

This all takes time. And you need to stay alive during the interim.

Large corporate clients are hard to sign up, but once they do, **they are very sticky.** The hassle of moving off your platform, onto a new untested provider can be material to their business. If your company provides a decent, reliable service, is true to your word on delivery, and works constructively on any issues that arise, then they will have a client for life and an evangelist in the market for your business.

Whatever model you choose, it is important in a B2B software business that for each medium sized client, you can see a path to **annual**

recurring revenue of at least $150,000 plus. This, of course, is a ball-park figure, but it is often the minimum number needed to make a vendor relationship work. Especially when you take account of the cost and length of client acquisition, implementation cycle, relationship management, and sale and client support.

This number **does not** need to be reached in year one. Often in year two, a client might reach $10,000 per month in license fee revenue. They will also likely have some additional consulting, training, and customization they need from you. You can charge for all that.

Long term, it is best to **keep consulting to about 20 percent maximum** of your monthly revenue per client. Many customers want a lot of hand holding and you will have an opportunity to charge them for this. However regular, contractual license revenue is much more reliable and increases your company valuation by an order of three times, compared to that of the "one-off" consulting work.

Some clients may want an **outsourced managed service** from you. That should be a separate discussion to the core contract license agreement. That model involves moving their work in-house for you to complete. This can make sense especially after a couple of years working together successfully, but it is a much wider relationship, with increased risk, operational, human resources, and managerial requirements. It will require a whole new contract and substantially higher fees being charged by you.

LUMS Software Pricing Model

Along the way you, will be asked to justify your pricing model. There is always someone in the room that will play the "devil's advocate" on your pricing proposal. It is often a failed entrepreneur who never even tried.

It can help to use a **LUMS model** to defend this. This divides the cost clients are charged for the solution across four different areas:

- **License fee**
- **User numbers**
- **Maintenance**
- **Support**

Plugging in these numbers in the early days gives you an idea of the cost of managing a client and what you will need for them to be economically viable. If they won't pay a fee in that range, you realize (over a number of years) then that they are not worth the trouble.

Some software companies charge additional fees for support. Some don't. Initially, we did—for support—outside normal European business hours. In the United States, we didn't (the market wouldn't bear the cost).

Having a detailed, salient response to queries on the pricing model is a great way to justify your charges and makes you look more credible and professional. It is what large software companies do all the time. It's also always handy to have this information on demand for potential investors.

Pricing for Your Series A Funding Round

As you start to think about your Series A round, you will be beginning to target much larger companies as prospective clients.

The aim here is to reach a **mid-six figure annual recurring revenue for each large marquee client**. Given the company's current size and the work involved in landing a global organization, you can probably manage about one of these guys per year. So, choose them carefully.

The Series A funding round will allow you to ramp this up. To be a successful high growth technology company, you will need to aim for mid-six figures annual revenue for each large client (i.e., $500,000—moving to above a million over time). That size of target client is the company with 50,000+ employees, in probably twenty-five locations across the world. They will likely use your software initially in one or two offices and have a clear plan to roll that out globally over the next year or two. It will take at least a year to land this client and cost you tens of thousands in client acquisition costs. They can make or break your business.

To make this worthwhile, when you get them over the line, you will need to charge at least $200,000 upfront. This can be structured as an initial POC (Proof of Concept—basically a test drive of the solution) fee of $100,000 and a further $100,000 paid after three to six months, as you onboard the first team and they go live.

Be warned, that many large global institutions have a fee threshold (in the finance industry, it is often $250,000), that once reached, kicks off a review at a "Global Cost Committee" level. You want to avoid this like the plague. They often only meet once a month or even only once per quarter and you can easily find yourself pushed into a nine-month waiting game that will kill your business and stop fundraising dead.

The VCs you meet for the Series A round will expect you to be on your way to landing one of these larger global clients (i.e., well engaged in the sales pipeline). The funding they provide will help to get that deal over the line. It should also help with resourcing the team you will need to replicate winning many more large organizations globally.

Conclusion

Price the technology, so you can "land and expand." If this has to be an initial $50,000 in Year 1, aim to have the solution rolled out the following year aiming for $150,000 annually (including license and support) for smaller clients and over $500,000 for large businesses.

Chapter Summary

- Business software is normally priced per client, per team, per user, or a mix of these.
- Best B2B Pricing Model is a high minimum threshold, with plenty of upside revenue potential, as the solution is rolled out across the company.
- For a seed round, aim for $150,000 annually for the initial reference client. It may take a couple of years to get there.
- For a Series A round, aim for $500,000 to $1 million annually for large global organizations. Each one of these will take at least a year to land.
- The LUMS pricing model can be useful in calculating suitable pricing and justifying your cost basis to potential clients.

CHAPTER 7

The First Client

Introduction

In a company that sells software to businesses, the first real paying client changes everything.

It's the initial stage of validation and "Product/Market Fit."

Start the business development cycle **long** before your MVP version is ready to be shown to anyone. It will take time to line up interested prospects and you can finalize your product development work in the meantime.

Aim for your first paying client to be a company that you already know in the industry. If you know the people working there and they respect you and you know their business, its challenges, and a bit about their internal processes, it makes signing them up much easier.

That is what I did. Our first client was a company I knew well. I had had coffee with some of the directors before. I knew some of their staff and had worked with them on previous projects. I was able to tell one of them about the product we were building, and he immediately recognized the need for it. When he had seen our MVP, he was able to contribute some fantastic ideas. And when we were ready, we conducted a series of demos over a few weeks at the company's office. The upshot, after a brief product trial, was that they asked us for a contract, and we signed a three-year license deal.

This deal didn't happen by accident. It happened because I successfully mined my professional network. Already being a credible thought leader in our industry and being well known by the market locally, it meant the process of convincing potential clients was that much easier and shorter. Not having a solid network and reputation can be a serious handicap for new technology start-ups.

Especially when they are led by people like me, who have never run a technology company before!

That first deal had to be approved by the head office in the United States. While that process slowed down the go-live date somewhat (it always does), because the initial license cost was borne solely by their European office, it meant we were able to conclude the deal in a few months.

It always takes at least a few months (often up to six) to find, convince, and deploy your solution at a medium sized company. Small players won't have the money to buy new business software. The mid-tier guys will have **both the budget and also the hunger** to move up to the "Top Tier" in their particular sphere. The easiest way for them to do that, and often the most cost-efficient investment, is through the use of innovative technology.

This means that finding your first paying business client should be done by either:

- **Working with an up and coming company you already know** and that respects your business knowledge and industry experience.
- Targeting a dynamic, fast growing, and hungry **mid-tier player** in your market segment. They have the pockets and appetite to look at new technology.

Cold calling B2B software does not work. It just annoys people. We all hate getting those calls. Save your time and energy in the early days and focus on the companies you know, in your space, close enough to you so that you can visit their offices regularly.

By all means **e-mail** or send some product details to your contacts across the industry on LinkedIn and **follow it up** with a phone call. But if you think you are going to secure your first decent sale from some faraway business that you do not know and who has never heard of you, I am afraid that is a pipedream.

No one buys expensive business software from people they don't know. Would you?

How an Angel Investor Can Help

You will have to **fund some further product development** once your first client starts to trial the solution. From the initial demos, they will immediately identify gaps in the product and a number of features that you will have to deliver, to get them over the line. The first client will be unlikely to pay much for a new, untested solution. They certainly won't pay for the product gaps needed to make it ready for real world deployment. This part of the process is about getting your product from a decent MVP to a real enterprise software solution that delivers value in the business world.

That's going to cost cash and you won't have much left. It is at this point that your **angel investor steps up**.

You will need **angel investment** to cover any development gaps identified by the first client, and also the operating costs just to keep the lights on. Simultaneously, as that first client is onboarding—and you must prepare for a long implementation process to make them referenceable and happy—you will be in intense funding discussions with seed VCs.

You will also be doing the next round of demos with the companies that become your **second and third clients**. It's a terribly busy time. Using your first client as leverage and their **testimonials** as evidence of your product value, you will be moving the next prospects solidly along your sales pipeline. That's why it's so important that the first client is delighted, and you should bend over backwards to make them so.

Your initial client will understand that they are the first real users of your software and that the company is tiny. That's why you will be **giving them a great deal.** This will allow some leeway, both in what is possible and also the time it takes you to do things. However, if your small size and responsiveness to their needs becomes a big issue over time and slows down their daily work, then you are going to have a huge problem.

Remember—**without a referenceable first client, you probably won't get a seed funding round.**

Most VCs will not touch you for seed funding until you have a decent paying business client. Perhaps they will in Silicon Valley, if you are on your fourth successful start-up, but back here in the "Real World," investors want to see your product validated in the industry by a reputable player.

One that is paying you some cold hard cash for your solution and waxing lyrically about the benefits it brings to their business.

Your first business client will likely be **geographically close** to you. Businesses don't take a chance on brand new technology companies with no clients that are hundreds of miles away. This means you should meet them in person as much as possible and demo the product to them **at their office**.

Future prospects will often do the first demo remotely, over Zoom or WebEx, and that's fine. But for the early clients, it needs to include some face-to-face as much as possible.

It's not just to ensure you win the deal. It is also so that you can watch the clients' body language, reactions in the room, register who is interested in the software, and who is bored. Perhaps you have been pitching your product to compliance managers, and unfortunately, they don't seem interested, but the head of operations is all over you and loves the product. You may have to realign the teams you are targeting. That kind of feedback comes over time and really helps inform your future business development strategy.

The B2B Business Development Cycle

The typical B2B business development cycle for the first client will look something like this:

1. Initial e-mail/call/coffee
2. First onsite demo
3. Second onsite demo with key decision makers
4. Product trial
5. Client onboarding

Arrange an **initial e-mail/call/coffee**, after a warm introduction from a colleague or friend in the industry. Tell the target client that you want to get their thoughts and feedback on the product you are building. Tell them that their input following a short demo would be invaluable. Make it clear this is not a sales meeting. Explain what your product does, the problem it is solving, and the key benefits you are delivering to the industry.

Prior to the first onsite meeting, speak to the organizer and find out who will attend, their role in the company, and as much as you can about their typical work processes. This will give you valuable insight into what to show them at the first meeting. A mutual friend or peer might also be able to provide some color on the reality of the company's current situation, specifically where its most significant business pain points lie. You need to conduct extensive research—their website, Google, press releases, online forums, industry events—to bring yourself up to speed with all the aspects of their business, as they could relate to your product. Going in to see them fully briefed will be appreciated and your little team will look professional. A first big prospect demo is just like an important job interview. Preparation is everything.

First Onsite Demo

Request access to the meeting room ten minutes before the meeting is due to start. This is an especially important time to get things quickly set up. This means arriving at the client's office at least twenty minutes early and dealing with security and sign in protocols.

You want to be ready, with your software on their big TV screen, for when the target client's team walks in the door. That way, you are straight into shaking hands, exchanging business cards, and doing the introductions.

Take the lead in this meeting. It's the easiest way to control it.

After the introductions, suggest to your key contact that you give a brief two-minute background on who you are and why you built the product. Then offer to run them through the "greatest hits" of your solution and have time for questions and next steps. This introduction is your chance to remind them that you come from their industry, have lived their pain for many years and are a seasoned professional and thought leader in this space. Remember, you were forced to build this software because you couldn't find it in the market.

Do the company introduction while your intern is fixing any last-minute technology, Wi-Fi, or connectivity issues. Many times, I have started the first demo meeting while the team was still trying to find the right socket to start the laptop. You may need to run the Wi-Fi off your phone if the guest Internet is bad. This became such a problem when we expanded into New York, that we ended up buying our own hotspot. I had to pay a $400 deposit as we had no credit history in the United States.

Plan and rehearse a **20-minute demo** of your product's "greatest hits." The **key benefits** of the solution to your client (as you understand them). TED talks are always 18 minutes for a reason. After that time, people's attention span naturally loses interest. It doesn't matter what you are selling or how good you are at pitching. You need to be wrapping up at the 20-minute mark and opening the floor to questions.

Have your solution updated with the prospect's logo and any public information you know about them (as appropriate) uploaded into the solution. You have to get them thinking like they are already using it. In the same way, a realtor dresses a house for sale, you must have the prospect imagining they are using your solution in **their** world.

We would always place our potential client's logo on our login page. Then set up some of the functionality to match the names of departments and even people within their business (if we knew their names). That's why it is so important to find out as much as possible about your target client before the meeting. Looking like you have really prepared, taking the time to upload some relevant dummy data, and making the product look like it's already deployed, can make a big difference.

Have someone else take lots of notes. You **can't** do a demo and run the meeting and take notes, and ensure all the key topics and core questions are covered. It is just not possible. You will do a sloppy job and miss something important. I know this from bitter experience.

Instead, have your intern set the software and hardware up. Get the cables in place and have them liaise with any internal technology staff. Make sure you have every type of connection and cable. We presented at the global headquarters of one of Europe's largest banks and there was no socket for an HDMI cable. Another time I used a brand-new Surface laptop and there was no USB port on the device. I had only bought it the day before and hadn't noticed.

The cost of all these different adapters and cables can be a few hundred dollars, but it is worth it. There is nothing worse than when technology lets you down at an important demo. It could easily be your prospect's poor Wi-Fi connection. But you can't blame them. You are a technology company, so have your technology in order. Otherwise you look like an amateur.

Toward the later third of the meeting, offer to work with them to update the solution with the details of their business and/or some dummy data that reflects their business "world." This is a straightforward way to get their conceptual agreement in place and allows the relationship to move forward to the next stage. No one is going to buy a new product on the strength of one meeting. Instead, at the first meeting, nail down an agreement for a second "deep dive" demo and reiterate it again at the end, when you complete a summary of next steps. This means you leave with concrete actions on which to work with them. It gradually brings them into your orbit and pours a solid foundation for the future relationship.

When the demo finishes and the prospect seems to run naturally out of questions, it is your turn. Have a few informed questions ready related to their internal businesses, their future corporate strategy, and the key projects they are currently working on. All this builds up your internal knowledge of their business. It will make it far easier to onboard if you understand their internal dynamics.

Follow up with a nice thank you e-mail, and any documentation or marketing material agreed. Confirm the date for the follow-up second meeting, and try and nail it down. Give them a couple of days to respond and then send a chaser e-mail. At more senior levels of staff, it can take a few days to align calendars and have a follow-up meeting confirmed. If you still do not hear back from them, give them a quick call to touch base. Keep it short and simple and find out their latest thoughts on the next steps.

Second Onsite Demo

No business client buys software on the strength of one demo. It will always take at least two, and often many more, to get them over the line. If the first demo was organized by your key client contact, the second demo will likely be attended by the key decision makers at the company. This will likely include the heads of different departments, and in the mid-size company you are targeting, it may also include a director.

If they have agreed to a second demo, it is because they are potentially interested and they want to see more. The feedback from the first meeting will have been positive. You now have to conduct a much deeper analysis of your product and how it can benefit them.

It can be hard to cover over any cracks in the product at this point, as they will be conducting a more granular review of the solution. You are better off being honest about what your product can't do, and the development gaps you both agree exist. As long as any product enhancements make sense for your market, then tell them that you are happy to work closely together to close them.

Show them a walkthrough of dummy data and information they have sent you, and how it would be set up and managed in the product. They will have lots of questions and the second meeting will likely last one to two hours. Some of this will be positive for you and some of it may be unpleasant. There is always someone in the room happy to pull you apart. Have your own questions ready for them too. It helps deflect a bulldog who has their teeth firmly into some perceived gap in your technology.

By now, they will be starting to ask questions around the software **commercials**. That is a great sign that they are getting serious. Make it clear, as the first client, that you are flexible on numbers and that what you are really interested in is a long-term mutually fruitful partnership. This partnership would be economically valuable for them and would enable them to have input into the final development of the product, so that it reflects their workflow and business requirements.

The message to empathize is that you will not let price stand in the way of doing a deal. In return, you want a testimonial that can be put on your marketing material and also a short video you will shoot, where they talk about their business and their honest opinion on using your product.

Offer a **trial** run as the first stage of integration and offer unlimited training and users to get them hooked onto the product. Offer to set up some test users and work with them on customizing their setup correctly. This trial or product "test drive" should be done over a tight defined period (e.g., three or four weeks) and should have a criterion for success agreed in advance. That is, you agree with the prospect that if the solution does what you promised, they will then commit to buying a license.

When they agree to a trial, sit down and work with them on their processes and workflow, documenting carefully what they currently do every day. Identify the pain points they have, why they feel your solution might help and then set up the software to address their issues. Pull in as much of their data now as they will allow you to touch. If you can replicate their workflow but it has their pain points removed (in a way that is more efficient or cheaper), then you are on a home run.

Even if they walk away after the trial, you will have gathered a ton of valuable information and insight about how real paying clients would use your solution; what worked great and what were the product gaps. Immediately set about fixing these issues and expanding the product, so as to start setting up your next prospect trial run. You need to find them fast, as you won't have much time before any angel funding runs out.

Closing the Deal

The final piece of the puzzle is reeling them in and getting them to sign a contract. This is the point where sometimes their early enthusiasm can slow down markedly. It always does when a company is being asked to get their check book out.

A number of objections will likely arise. You need to systematically address and remove them. The procurement department may believe you are too small, that you have no funding to keep going, that the cost is too high, or have concerns that you can't support them if they roll the product out globally.

Have answers ready for each of these objections. You are a fast-growing company with investors lined up to fund you. You are experts in the industry and understand their business inside out. You will be charging subsequent clients a far higher license fee. You are targeting scaling capital to be able to support clients globally and you have already started the recruitment process in other time zones. It is all about having a credible response to these pushbacks and demonstrating that you are a reputable software vendor.

Financial pushback may occur. Every business wants a bespoke software solution, they just don't want to pay for it. Tell them they do not have to pay the trial fee **if** they don't go forward with the product.

Tell them that if they do go forward, you will discount the trial fee from their Year 1 software license. That way there is no risk to them financially and you have significantly de-risked a contract.

While this kind of commercial structure is not ideal, you need to **be creative** with your first client and make it easy for them to say yes. You won't have to offer a deal like this in your home country again. However, you may have to offer a sweetheart deal overseas when you start to target new countries and expand.

Really try and get the client to agree to **at least pay something for the trial**. Even $5,000 would be great. That way you can go to the seed VCs you are targeting and tell them that you have a strong prospect engaged in a paid pilot of the solution. It is not a paying client, but it is a great sign of product value.

The revenue from client number one will be small anyway. It certainly won't be enough to keep your business alive and pay salaries to the expanding team. That is what the angel funding can do. However, the small amount of revenue from this first client makes you a **revenue generating company** and that has real value. You are looking at a valuation of a few million dollars. Especially if there is a clear path to revenue growth with the client over the next few years. Ideally, they will sign a multi-year license contract, while you are also working on closing a pipeline of similar companies in the industry. Investors will eat this up.

It can be a shock when the first client calls you and asks for a contract. When this happened to me, I didn't have one. I paid $50 for a standard B2B SaaS software contract template online. Then I reviewed and changed anything I thought was incorrect. I updated the financial numbers in the contract schedule at the back, held my breath, and sent it to the client to review.

Finalizing the contract always delays things further. It is far better to **offer to use the client's standard contract** and negotiate backwards with them on that. Most of these contracts are boiler plate but you as a small company need to ensure you can match their support requirements, business hour coverage, and turnaround time for updates, bugs, and support issues.

Ensure that your **implementation is allowed to proceed unimpeded** while the contract is being negotiated. Contract discussions will probably begin as the trial comes to an end and you do not want to lose momentum on the full implementation, or both teams laying down tools while the legal matters are sorted out. Most decent companies won't want to do this either and a good relationship with your client will ensure that the ball keeps rolling on the implementation project.

The sweetheart deal you will have to offer this first client should be time limited with a regular pricing review, ideally at the end of Year 1. The client won't like this, but you can agree to limit any upward price changes to (say) 20 percent in Year 2. This will make it more palatable for them long term and easier to get internal budget approval.

It also means that not only are you now a revenue producing technology company, you also have **a multi-year license deal in place with scaling revenue** over the next few years, from a referenceable reputable company. That's a good growth story for a seed VC investor to fund.

All the issues and objectives raised in this section can be overcome by having a great partnership with your first client. B2B software sales—just like raising investor funding—is very much a relationship-based business.

Onboarding the First Client

Run the trial period **as if it is the first phase of implementation**. This helps gain their conceptual agreement that they will be fully onboarding to the product shortly. The prospect will look to you completely to manage the onboarding process. As you will never have done one before, it can be tricky to manage. The key is to build an **initial implementation plan** that specifies each of the key steps in the process, underlying tasks across each area, suggested dates for completion and owners assigned to each task.

Get ahead of them on this and produce a first draft quickly. Send them the initial draft and ask them to update it from their perspective. You will have had to assign some tasks to them. That's ok. It's a point for discussion at the implementation calls. I recommend at least two calls a week. One to plan the week ahead and another to review progress. If the client is highly engaged, there will also be a steady stream of emails during the week. Try and visit their offices at least once a week. It is better to conduct one of the two weekly meetings on site. You can also use that visit for initial training, user set up and to answer any of their (likely many) questions.

Accept now to yourself that during this implementation process, **the client may become unhappy at some point.** Your team is new, you are all learning, and there will be bugs in the product that may annoy your client and threaten to upset the whole software trial. You will be much better equipped and experienced at subsequent implementations.

These **test drives are often extended.** Sometimes substantially. The client identifies a number of issues or insists on a new feature before they will go live. With the first client, you may just have to suck it up and agree. That's what the angel funding is for.

On a positive note, if they insist on new functionality before signing the contract, it is actually a validation that they want to use the product and see real value in it. Take this to the VCs you are courting and tell them that closing these urgent product gaps is exactly why you need seed funding quickly.

The key message for your first full implementation is to **take your time.**

This is easier said than done as you will burn through your angel cash in no time, but it is still essential to get the first client implementation right.

It is essential you transform the MVP from a three wheeled car to a reliable SUV (the Ferrari can wait till next year). That is, **the scalable, easily deployable solution you can deploy repeatedly worldwide.** The gaps you need to build, the time it takes the client to get setup, the post-trial approval and agreement on the contract, all take a lot of time. Far longer than you thought. That's ok. It will be much faster next time around. Your team will be implementation experts in no time. Your mission as CEO is to stay in business that long.

Now that you are finishing the first implementation, it is time to agree to that **reference** they promised. It should be part of the contract you agree with them. You need to be allowed to put them on your website and all marketing material, and the quote should be a measurable benefit the product brought to their business. For example, "This solution increased our efficiency overnight by 40 percent and reduced our overheads by $2 million dollars a year."

Have this client agree to produce a joint **"Client Case Study."** This is a short marketing brochure on how they use your product. We did a number of these studies and clients used them for their business development and we did too. It was "win win." They looked like they were using new cutting-edge software and we looked like we had a wider client base. Send it fair and wide to your full mailing list and especially all those VCs that won't answer your calls.

Conclusion

Your first client and their successful onboarding turns you from an early stage MVP start-up, to an income generating software company. You won't make much money on the first deal, but the experience to your team and your insight into future product development will be invaluable. Lastly, it enables you to face VC investors for the first time in some confidence and look for your seed funding round, to move you to the next level.

Chapter Summary

- Start the business development process immediately after the MVP is built.
- Learn the typical B2B business development cycle.
- Expect it to take three to six months to land the first business client.
- Complete a detailed product "gap analysis" with the first client.
- Consider angel funding to bridge any cashflow and product development shortfall.
- Be prepared to offer a "sweetheart" deal to the first client.
- Push for a three-year license deal, with annual upward only pricing reviews.
- Take the lead on implementation and onboarding.

CHAPTER 8

Fundraising

Introduction

This is one of the most important chapters in the book. To scale quickly, first locally and then globally, you will need cash. A lot of cash.

If you are selling B2B software, the procurement cycle can be extremely lengthy and then there is often a long wait to get paid. This means you will need to raise cash to fund your operating costs and finance company expansion.

The three typical funding rounds that lead up to a $10 million valuation are as follows:

- **Angel investment**—Often $50,000 to $100,000 early stage investment from a high net worth individual. Might be more. Unlikely to be less.
- **Seed funding**—From a professional Venture Capital (VC) firm and typically between $500,000 and $1 million.
- **Series A funding**—A larger round of $2+ million from a VC firm to start scaling the business globally. The size of these rounds has increased (often dramatically) in recent years.

The start-up capital you inject in the company as the CEO and founder, is for putting the first pieces of the jigsaw together. It is about building a good MVP and starting to find the right people you need to run and market the company.

Angel investment is to keep you alive while you secure and then successfully deploy the solution at your first paying client. It gives you credibility with VCs and allows you some breathing room, while you get the product market-ready.

Seed funding allows you to expand the initial team that you will need to grow, from this first client and then onboard a few more companies. It also allows you to start becoming serious about targeting big worldwide players, as well as taking the first tentative steps to expand the business globally.

Series A is for scaling your product worldwide. You will now have product/market fit, some growing revenue, and a few reputable, smaller clients. This funding enables you to expand the core team and ramp up resources at home and at new overseas offices. It provides the runway and capital you need to seriously challenge the technology market leaders and bring home a couple of mega deals with the global titans in your niche.

Other start-up experts may have different views on the rationale behind each of these funding rounds and the use and timing of receiving the money, but in my experience as a start-up CEO, this is broadly what the funding is used for.

You are always thinking about your next funding round, even before the current deal is closed.

Generally speaking, the valuation of the company will increase four to five times (referred to as "4x to 5x") at each funding round. It may be less, it may be more. In this ballpark is what investors will expect. While there are some exceptions to this depending on the market (e.g., MedTech—it can take $100 million to develop a new drug), these multiples are broadly correct.

Most angels will look to invest at a valuation well below $1 million. This means an angel might invest $75,000 at a $500,000 Pre-Money Valuation ("PMV," i.e., before investment). The seed VC might look to put in $500,000 at a PMV of $2,500,000. Finally, the Series A investor would invest $2 million at a PMV somewhere north of $10 million.

Our angel invested $60,000 at a valuation of roughly $400,000, which equated to selling approximately 15% of the equity in the business. Our seed VC invested nearly $1 million at a PMV of $3.5 million and our Series A Term sheet was at a PMV of $10 million.

It is important to understand this typical valuation cycle. It will help get you into the investor's mindset and also allows you as the CEO to work backwards; targeting the kind of revenue you need to achieve, to reach each valuation point (in the case of B2B IT companies, that is roughly ten times recurring revenue), and secure the next funding round.

Finding Your First Angel Investor

Remember that fundraising is like dating—if you come across as desperate, no one will want to touch you.

It takes time to find a suitable partner and you should start your fundraising activities as soon as your MVP is in a decent shape.

To go after your first external investor, you will need to do three things:

1. Market the company to a pool of potential target investors.
2. Put together a cracking investor deck and practice pitching it repeatedly.
3. Write a business plan for the company and its future plans.

Marketing to Investors for the First Time

Research online the investors that look at your particular industry. They are not that hard to find.

Buy a database of investors and VCs that invest in your market segment. We used free ones we found online but paid options were available for less than $150. We also used a good matching service (that cost about $50) that allowed you to input details of the company, current revenue, where you were in the start-up process, and fed back to us the investors in the United States and Europe that looked at companies like us at seed stage of development. There are a number of these options available online.

Many countries and geographical areas have VC industry boards (e.g., Irish Venture Capital Association, New England Venture Capital Association, etc.). Find their members on the website and analyze if any of them would look at your space and a seed size of investment.

Make a list of the Top 20 VCs who might invest in your seed round. Start with the ones located close to you and then add them on LinkedIn.

While they won't always accept your connection, you have to try. If you are a thought leader in your space and you already have some common connections, then they probably will. Write a nice invitation note telling them you are not looking for money right now but just to connect.

Sometimes it's a good idea to add someone else in the company first (i.e., not an investment decision maker) and go from there. I often did this (e.g., adding a Head of Operations or Technology) and after they would accept, I was able to contact an Investment Director while already having a connection at the company. It made establishing contact much easier.

Do not accept any funding from an investor who tries to link providing cash to reaching specific milestones of development. This might include receiving a chunk of funding when you sign a client or start a product pilot. Some investors try and do this, and it is not worth the hassle for you. It is an additional source of stress you do not need. Investors should get out of your way and let you do your thing. If they don't trust you enough to do that, then why are they funding you?

Your First Investor Deck

Pulling your first investor deck together is actually pretty straightforward. The investor deck is an updated version of the first company deck you put together (in Chapter 1).

The difference is that you update it from the perspective of a VC investor. The most important thing to have in your mind, is to have up front and central, **how they will make money out of you**.

The key points to address are:

- What will you do with the cash?
- What are the projected revenues over the next three years?
- What exciting deals you are working on right now?
- Any recent company traction, for example, awards, media coverage, deals closed, and so on?
- What is the exit plan for the business, that is, how will they make a profit from investing?

Emphasize the size of the total addressable market globally. Do not put something stupid like $5 trillion or $800 billion. You need to have a niche targeted and a source for the projected future size of the space (find it on Google).

Highlight the severe pain in the industry and how your research and own experience demonstrates that potential clients are screaming out for your product. You are a recognized expert in your space, and you tried to find the software and couldn't—you were **forced** to build it. You know the industry inside out. You have a huge network and are a credible vendor with a professional reputation. You are pushing an open door. All you are missing is the funding to press the accelerator and blast off.

Add a slide that shows the existing competitors in the space and state clearly why your product is superior (higher quality, faster, cheaper, etc.). Don't be afraid of the competition. Love your competition. They will make you great. A fast-growing market space consisting of multiple innovative start-ups will give you the motivation you need to strive hard to be ahead of the pack. That is a great position to be in.

Keep to the 10 slides structure we outlined in the first chapter, and practice pitching it relentlessly.

Your First Business Plan

Around this time, you will need to pull together a business plan. Some seed VCs (and even angels) will insist upon it and some won't. It makes sense to have one ready to send to them when discussions get serious. Once investor negotiations advance, someone will want to see a business plan (wouldn't you?).

Treat it as an opportunity to put down in detail for the first time, the company, the market, how you plan to conquer it, and the financials behind it. The business plan is a projected road map. That is all. Everyone knows that the projections and plans you document will change significantly as you expand. That's ok. It is an evolving document. The important thing is that you have thought strategically about the future and have the operational plan.

A typical Business Plan may run anywhere from 25 to 40 pages.

A suggested template format for a seed funded focused business plan is as follows:

1. Executive Summary covering the following five areas:
    - The Product
    - The Market
    - The Strategy
    - The Company
    - Financials
2. Business Overview
3. Market Opportunity
4. Industry and Competition
5. Product Proposition and Key Progress to Date
6. Marketing Plan
7. Management Team
8. Operations and Legal
9. Key Risks
10. Revenue and Pricing Model
11. Ownership and Structure
12. Financial Projections and Key Assumptions
13. Overview of Financial Projections
14. Funding to Date
15. Exit Strategy
16. Conclusion

Appendices:
1. Team Biographies
2. Product Screenshots

Angel Funding

The $30,000 I proposed to build a decent MVP will not get you far, especially when it comes to giving up the day job and focusing on getting that first client full time. That's why you need angel funding. The $50,000 or $100,000 they can bring to the table, can be the difference between life and death for a start-up at this stage of expansion.

The angel investor will probably want somewhere between 10% and 15% of the business for their investment. They will probably be a wealthy individual; either someone you know, a friend of a friend, or an entrepreneur in the industry that had a successful exit and now invests in new start-ups.

Many countries have good angel networks that even host regular pitching sessions for companies like yours, direct to their members. If they are interested in providing some funding, they will often nominate one of their members with direct experience of growing a business in the space to be your mentor. They can provide funding quickly and the legal and documentation process is quick and easy.

For the angel investor, their investment is largely an informed lottery ticket. They know the chance of you making it is slim but if they can see the potential, they can add significant value to the business through their knowledge, expertise, and networks. The mentoring a good angel will give you, as a first time CEO, is invaluable.

The VC Mindset

Before we look at the seed round, it is vital to **understand the VC mindset** and put yourself in their position.

What return is the VC targeting in their investments (probably approx. 10x, i.e., ten times return)? Where are their funds in their investment cycle and what size of check do they normally write? How long does it take them to make an investment decision and when will they want their money back (typically five years and sometimes as long as seven)?

Remember a VC might invest in ten companies like yours. It expects **seven to completely fail.** Two will roughly break even and they will receive the original investment back. The remaining one (you!) needs to be a great success and make a huge return, to cover all the other losses in their fund and provide **their** investors with a great return (given that their cash will probably be tied up for five to seven years).

The first question an investor will ask you is **how you** will make money. The second question they will ask you is **how they** will make money. Put yourself in their shoes. Your business is your baby, but they see a hundred businesses a week.

Future potential is what drives your valuation at all stages of fundraising—angel, seed, and Series A. However, there is an important **difference in the perspectives of the U.S. and European VCs.**

- **The European VCs** and investors tend to be more conservative and value your business by looking at the **current** revenues and what you have achieved to date.
- **The U.S. VCs** are future oriented and will value your business based on the **future** growth opportunity and whether you are the right team to deliver on it.

This difference in perspective—the European past orientated and the U.S. future orientated—is a key distinction to become acquainted with and to help you decide where you want to raise money.

For a new start-up business, to me, this is a no-brainer. If possible, you want to raise money from the US Venture Capital industry. They will drive you hard—extremely hard, but they will bring you a huge amount of credibility globally. They will have a massive network they can plug you into, to support your growth in the United States, as well as mentors and advisors they know, that can act as a guide (often in-house). They will expect you to have a U.S. company, so **set up a "Delaware C Corp"** if you are from overseas, and they will want **Preference Shares**, not the Ordinary Shares that you as the founder holds.

The "**herd mentality**" of Venture Capital investors is insane. They speak at the same events and the same conferences. They all want to be the first to find the latest new, shiny thing and get in early on the most exciting game-changing technology. You need to set yourself up, through your marketing and social media, as that new shiny thing. Once you are fixed in their mind like this, you will have no problem finding institutional investor funding.

The VC will want to **build a relationship with you over some time**. And so, they should. No one gives $1 million to someone they don't know and don't trust. I wouldn't give me $1 million without getting to know me and I wouldn't expect anyone else to either. Take your time, meet in person, speak to potential VCs regularly, send them your latest traction and marketing collateral, and tag them on your LinkedIn posts.

They will get to know and trust you over a few months and that makes everything so much easier.

Remember raising money is like buying a house. The first time you buy a house you might not have a clue about mortgages or all the legal terms. The language is all new to you and you don't know how the processes work. You are all worried about getting ripped off. The fourth house you buy, you know exactly what should happen, the legal work involved, and how not to get fleeced by the other party. It's the exact same with raising VC funding. The first time you do it you will be clueless. After raising money from multiple institutional investors and perhaps a couple of bridge rounds (covered in Chapter 11), you will be much more informed and relaxed, as a seasoned fundraising pro.

The Seed Funding Round

Now you are targeting the big boys. The real professional VC investors. Getting one of them onboard is hard. Extremely hard. But it can be done.

Remember the golden rule— **"traction trumps everything."**

If you have good traction, a business starting to grow quickly, excitement generated in the market, and a good team to deliver the strategy, you **will** find seed investment.

Organize a few coffees, online calls and demos, and then get serious. A junior member of the team will scout the market. Get to know them over time. Keep them updated on your key news and wins. Send all related marketing news to them regularly.

The relationship will evolve over a few months. It most certainly won't happen overnight.

The VC will want to see that you are coming good on the initial plan you told them about. For example, that first client you said you are signing up. That you are actually doing the trial and they are converting to full implementation. That story makes sense to them and they can see clearly you will need funding to keep growing.

When you do meet with VCs, **ask them lots of questions.** This will surprise them. They are not used to it. It shows you are serious about finding the right long-term investing partner and not just another desperate start-up screaming for money before they sink (it doesn't matter that you are!).

Let them justify why they should be your investment partner. What can they bring to the table? You need to pitch to them confidently and with a feeling of urgency. They should leave your meeting with a clear sense that the train is leaving the station and if they are not on it, they are going to miss out on a once in a lifetime investment opportunity.

When a VC is potentially happy to move forward, they will give you a **"Term Sheet"** to review.

That is a relevantly short document (typically five to ten pages), that details the investment they are willing to make into the company.

It is **not** a commitment. They still have to do due diligence but based on the accuracy of what you have told them in the pitches and meetings, if it all stands up, then these are the terms under which they will invest.

Think of a Term Sheet like receiving "Approval in Principle" from a bank for a loan or mortgage. The bank is saying that if all the information they request stacks up, then they will advance the funding. It is the same thing with a Term Sheet.

Once you receive a Term Sheet, you will need a specialized and experienced lawyer to negotiate on your behalf and explain the deal structure and terms. For most people, the largest financial engagement they are ever involved in, is buying a house. For a first-time entrepreneur, it will likely be the seed round.

Your seed round will probably be for somewhere between $500,000 and $1 million. Quite frankly, **it will have to be,** if you want to stay in business long enough to convert a few more clients and build out the team.

Not only will you have to pay your lawyers legal fees, but the VC investing will also be expecting that you pay their fees too. This is obviously unfair but is completely standard in the industry. Ask your VC to cap the fees at a specific amount (for example $15,000). If they are a decent, reputable firm, they will agree to do that. No VC wants a material portion of their funding going to the lawyers. They want it to be spent on scaling your business and increasing the value of their investment.

Ballpark, for legal fees, you are unlikely to see much change from $25,000 to $30,000. Our VC had a cap in place with their lawyers (they did plenty of deals), that was reasonable and greatly appreciated. A good VC that's on your side, knows that screwing you on legal fees just depletes working capital and is counterproductive.

At seed level, you are probably selling in the region of 20 percent of the company to your VC. This is pretty standard. Certainly, don't sell more than 25 percent. It will dilute you so much, that future rounds will leave you owning a ridiculously small stake in your business. A good VC wants you to sweat blood and tears on the company and they know you won't do that, if you haven't got a decent piece of the pie.

At this point, many VCs will insist on carving out an **Employee Share Option Plan** (called an ESOP) before they invest their cash. The size of this pool could be as low as 5 percent of the company shares to as high as 15 percent. This means, at the seed stage, the founders get diluted **twice**—for both the shares sold to the VC and the shares created and allocated to the ESOP (probably approx. 30 percent in total).

The ESOP should be awarded to your core management team and some held back for future company employees. It is pretty common to vest the shares to them over a three-year period. It is also common to revisit and expand the ESOP when you reach Series A funding time. This helps motivate the wider global team you will be recruiting at that point.

The amount of time it takes to close a seed round can be shocking. It took me about nine months to close our seed round. This was particularly long, but four to six months is common. At that time, you will be onboarding clients, trying to survive on your angel funding, and interviewing new staff to bring on once the funding closes.

It is an incredibly stressful period and the deal will take up a huge amount of your time as the CEO.

Managing the Stress

The start-up CEOs that make it, versus the start-up CEOs that don't, are the ones that are personally resilient enough to manage the near intolerable level of stress you may now be under. It is a horrible time in your life.

The business is actively running out of cash. You are probably starting the first client implementation and may need to begin more hiring. The days to bankruptcy are ticking down horribly in front of your eyes.

The initial team probably knows there is little money left and how important it is that you secure funding quickly.

Try to keep cool and keep your head during this time. It is extremely stressful and easier said than done.

If you survive this process, without a breakdown in your mental health, then congratulations—you are fit to be a start-up CEO.

Very few businesspeople experience the level of stress that comes with your job and this particular phase within it. You will probably start to resent reading articles about the supposedly "legendary" managers of large companies, that have actually never taken a risk with their own money or put their head on the chopping block. I know I do.

You will meet investors that recognize the value of your product, then try and rip you off because they know you are desperate. I had an early investor try to buy 51 percent of the company for $250,000. Of course, I turned him down. Then a year later when we were raising a bridge round, he got in touch again. I enjoyed telling him we had no space in the round and the company valuation was now $6 million.

Conclusion

Funding takes up **so** much time. Finding it, securing it, and then locking down the financials. It is a shock to most CEOs—the amount of time involved. You will be an expert after the seed round. Series A will be easier. You will know what to expect.

Chapter Summary

- Build a great investor deck and practice it repeatedly.
- Constantly refine the pitch based on investor feedback.
- Target angel funding while you secure and onboard the first client.
- Target seed funding from a VC to fund further expansion.
- Understand the VC mindset and their investment strategy.
- Start thinking about international expansion.
- Target Series A funding to build a global team, which can win the large global players in your industry.

CHAPTER 9

Building a Team of Trusted Advisors

Introduction

A great team of "trusted advisors" can turbo charge the growth of the company.

By "trusted advisor" I mean the collection of accountants, lawyers, advisors, and mentors you will need to engage, to successfully scale the business globally.

It is also easier than you think to build this network. Everyone wants to work with exciting new, fast growing technology companies. Your exciting vision for the business should be rammed down everyone's throat. It is not a matter of **if** you are going to be huge, but **when** you are going to be huge.

In particular, a good team of trusted advisors will help you scale the business far easier when it comes to managing international growth. This is because they can use their network and expertise to guide you globally, make warm introductions and recommendations, as well as assist with local regulation and compliance.

We will look at each in turn. How to find great advisors, what to expect them to do, and how to manage thorny pricing conversations.

Finding World Class Advisors

As in all things business, personal recommendations are the best. If you know someone who has grown a tech start-up and you respect them, they are the first port of call you should ask. They will also probably be more open to a candid discussion on commercials, the actual quality of service and the value received.

Attend a few "Meetup" events in your niche or for start-up businesses in the local area. Ask the speakers for recommendations. Ask the people you network with. You guys are all in the same boat. If they don't know who can help you, they may know someone who can.

Alternatively, approach the companies you admire and ask them who they use for their accounting and legal representation. Look on their websites, if you haven't got a direct contact or if they won't tell you. It's not that hard to find. They are often listed online, or you can do a Google search.

Post a "Start-up looking for accountants/lawyers, etc." question onto one of the LinkedIn groups in your area. Better still, repost your question into one of the start-up specific LinkedIn groups that exist in each country/city. Some of these global groups have hundreds of thousands of members and regional groups often have tens of thousands.

Ask for references from whoever responds. Look them up online and have a look at their reviews, from both clients and employees. Take the time to speak to the references provided. A fifteen minute phone call—understanding the range and quality of services they offer, how they charge, and their invoicing period (crucial in the early years)—can save you a mountain of pain later, if you are let down while trying to scale.

You need to have advisors that specialize in your space—FinTech, MedTech, SpaceTech, and so on. These guys know your area and have a great network. They provide huge value over the short and long term. They also understand in-depth regulatory and compliance requirements you must follow, in both your home country and internationally.

Your advisors are a resource. Use them. What does that new piece of U.S. or EU regulation mean for you? Ask them. They will have a view. If not, they are probably part of a global network that can find out. That way you will have a detailed answer on the latest news in your industry for your clients and investors.

Accountants

A good accountant can take a lot of your "red tape" pain away. They can keep and produce clear financial accounts, balance sheets, manage the business receipt process, produce Management Accounts for investors, process payroll and employment taxes, and even manage corporate governance (board meetings, minutes, AGMs, proxy voting, etc.). If you don't understand any of this stuff, they can take the time to explain it to you in a way that will make sense.

As soon as your business gets traction and certainly post-angel investment (and pre-seed round), find and engage a good accounting firm and begin the process of migrating to their systems (software, operations, and personnel). There is some work involved in this, but it is incredibly worthwhile, as it allows you to focus on growing your business, and not the endless cycle of red tape, taxation, and accounting filings. The accountants should also be set up so that they manage all payroll, tax returns, and related payments. This means your company will have independently produced accounts and independently managed payroll and tax returns. This is what professional investors want to see.

A small accounting firm is fine, as long as they know your space and can plug into their professional services network globally, as you expand. These are the guys who will be hungry for your business. The leading top and mid-tier accounting firms won't want to know you, until you are at a Series A stage of growth.

When I was growing one of my businesses, I asked locally who the best accounting firm for start-up software companies was. That list narrowed very quickly after some initial phone calls. It wasn't hard to find who understood the business and was prepared to discount their fees substantially in year one, for the benefit of a long term, fruitful financial partnership.

I have always emphasized to investors that I was removed from the whole payroll and taxation process (except for a final review), and that it was solely calculated, submitted, and paid by an independent accounting firm. That is what professional investors expect from professional companies.

It pays to think of clean reliable accounts, managed and delivered by an independent recognized accounting firm, as an asset and distinct competitive advantage to the business.

It's one of the first things an institutional investor will want to see, when they get serious about investing. It will be the **very first** thing an interested third party will want to see if you are considering an exit (and once you are successfully in scaling mode, you will be approached).

Proceed with your accountants as if you are being formally audited, even if an audit is not required in your country for a company of your size. This will have you running a tight final ship from early on and make more complex financial growth easier to digest, as the figures become larger.

Lastly, hand over the management of the company's corporate governance to a third party, ideally to your accountants. Any decent small or mid-size accounting firm should be able to offer this service. It is an invaluable delegation and will save you an immense amount of time trying to stay on top of the bureaucratic roundabout.

Lawyers

Finding technology focused business lawyers is not that difficult. The key is to find firms that will help small, start-up emerging businesses and structure their rate sheet accordingly.

You will be so busy keeping the company alive, onboarding your first decent client and meeting potential investors, that when you receive your first Term Sheet, you may be surprised to be asked by the VC, who are your lawyers (I know I was)?

That's the time to engage the best legal firm you can afford. To find a great firm, I had an advisor and investor in the company introduce me to a fast-growing mid-tier firm in Dublin. One that specialized in business law and had a history of negotiating start-up funding deals, with deep links into the local investor network.

Crucially, the partners had previously advised VCs on their Term Sheets and structuring their investment agreements. Nowadays, they were working for start-up businesses like my own. This "**poacher turned game-keeper**" legal representation was invaluable, when it came to detailed discussions of the funding offers we received. What was reasonable, what could we push back on, and what needed to go into the contract; plenty of things I had never even heard of!

Lastly, our lawyers were able to tell us that, on balance and based on their deep funding experience, our seed round agreement was fair and balanced for all the parties.

In Europe and APAC, the role of a lawyer is **different from that in the United States**. Most people in Europe deal with a lawyer when they are buying a house or dealing with a will. It is strictly focused on the legal ramifications of a particular transaction.

It is important to understand that lawyers in the United States hold a different, and from your perspective, a far more valuable role for you.

Think of the U.S. lawyers as your American **"business advisors."** They are not charging $700 an hour to simply review your legal documents. They will introduce you to their network, for potential clients and investors. If they focus on your space, this can be extremely valuable indeed.

The U.S. lawyers organize regular industry events at their offices and it is not that hard to hustle your way onto one of their panels. They are also often happy to speak at your industry events too and I organized this successfully on multiple occasions in New York.

Business Advisors

An advisor is someone who can add value to the business through their network, expertise, and experience.

Experienced and even retired experts in the field are often keen to become advisors to exciting new businesses in your industry. It keeps their finger on the pulse of the market and gets them excited. After a lifetime in your software segment, their network can be immense and invaluable. Ask them who they can introduce you to? This is a great way to get to the actual buyer (i.e., the very senior person) in the companies to whom you are selling.

At the earliest stages of your business, you will have no money to pay anyone. Advisors can be paid at a later date or optionally in some shares in the business.

When you appoint a new business advisor, put out a nice press release on social media and have them add the position on LinkedIn. Interview them for a thought leadership piece and let the world know they are joining your company in an advisory capacity. These should be well known and respected industry veterans, who will guide you in company expansion and bring credibility to the business.

Do not put business advisors on your board of directors' pre-VC funding. It is too early. This is something you can start to look at much later, when you begin thinking about Series A and the composition of your board becomes much more important. It is at that point that the name of a well-known expert in your field can demonstrate real value and provide investor credibility for a multimillion-dollar fundraising round.

Other types of advisors can be useful for specific requirements. For example, human resource advisors can be useful (and cost effective) to make sure employee contracts are up to date (e.g., GDPR in Europe) and that you comply with local law as you expand overseas.

Partnerships

A business partnership might be you agreeing with a large consulting or advisory company that you will jointly market and implement the software to their client base. This could involve creating a joint marketing document, agreeing to a revenue share, and promoting your alliance on social media and in the industry press.

The value of a partnership to you is credibility. It raises your profile as an up and coming player and can put the company on many investor radars (believe me they are watching!). This means you can get a higher funding valuation. A good partnership will increase the company's value.

For small start-ups, the quality of the relationship with the partners' key personnel is vital. Agreeing to a partnership can take a long time, and in the interim, people can resign and move on or take time out from their careers. All of this can badly set back the implementation of your partnership.

If you find a willing partner that puts its resources behind your agreement, the benefits can be substantial. As well as a new source of revenue, the partnership will enable you to leverage their marketing and business development resources, as well as their likely large global footprint. You can organize marketing events together, write joint white papers, and publish regular marketing collateral. The credibility of partnering with a leader in your industry will make it easier to raise finance and find new clients.

The problem with many of these "Joint Ventures" (JV) and partnership type agreements is that the small company ends up doing most of the work. You can get stuck in endless "cadence" meetings with the larger company and it can be hard to get them to make an actual decision.

However, on balance, a partnership with a name global business is a great way to get your company out there. Just don't expect too much revenue from it in Year 1 (if any). There are probably a lot of companies like you vying for their attention.

Chapter Summary

- A great team of "trusted advisors" can turbo charge the growth of the company.
- Ask companies you admire and the industry peers regarding who they recommend for accounting and legal services.
- Negotiate hard on fees in the early years, with a view to a long-term partnership as you expand.
- Find company advisors in the global markets you wish to target.
- Advisors will not be paid in the early years but should be very experienced, with a great network, and be keen to spread the word about the company to their peers.
- Consider industry partnerships with well-known companies if they increase your profile and may lead to good revenue growth over time.

PART III

CHAPTER 10

Personal Resilience

Introduction

Everything is your fault. Get used to it

All the problems facing the company, the financial burdens, unhappy clients, impatient investors, and exhausted employees, are yours and yours alone to bear. There is no one else coming to your rescue.

The start-ups process is called "**The Struggle**" for this very reason.

Other businesspeople don't understand. Employees don't understand. Your spouse doesn't understand. Neither do your kids or friends. You are stepping into a world of responsibility that very few people get to (or dare to) experience. It is all on you.

You are responsible for paying your employees, ensuring they have the money to meet their mortgage, and pay their kids' hospital bills. Paying your suppliers and making sure there is food on the table for your family. Meeting investors' targets and keeping tetchy clients happy. When anything at all goes wrong, the buck always stops with you.

It is the burden of this responsibility, often for years on end, more than any other part of the entrepreneurial journey, that **can't be mentored away or outsourced or delegated or shared**. It is you as the founder, and you alone, who has to carry this burden.

It is a really horrendous way to live and not one that can be carried on long term, without having serious personal consequences. But guess what? You may have to.

So, how do you manage the maelstrom and not have a nervous breakdown from the stress?

You have to develop solid mental and emotional coping strategies for being in a near constant state of bankruptcy and crisis. You learn to use that energy to make good business decisions, or at least be able to do business.

It is a tough process and it is **learned on the job. While you are in charge.** There is no flight simulator that can train you for the stress of growing a technology business, from an idea into a successful company. It is all real time, every time. It won't be a bumpy landing you face but the perfect storm of personal and corporate bankruptcy.

You have to get used to living **hours away from total financial collapse.** If you can't learn to exist like this for at least the first couple of years, then you are in the wrong game. The financial rewards and personal satisfaction can be immense but get yourself ready to be tested in a way you never thought possible.

The good news is that you can work your way through this. The way to eat an elephant is one bite at a time. You will learn to manage each crisis, one at a time, so you don't become overwhelmed. Good project management skills are essential and gaining them is a worthwhile investment of your time.

The start-up entrepreneur has **four key stakeholders** in their life that they are trying to simultaneously manage. This includes their personal life, investors, clients, and employees.

In the first few years of the business, it is exceedingly difficult to keep each plate of this "Entrepreneur's Quadrant" in the air. Managing it is a formidable balancing act.

Managing Your Personal Life

Having a solid personal and family foundation can do wonders to help armor your resilience, for the down days and regular knock backs.

Don't kid yourself. There is **no "off" switch** when you are a start-up CEO. Your default, resting thought will be, "how will I meet next week's payroll?" It will be like that for years. Your partner will know you're not present. Resentments can seethe. Acrimony is often the result, and it takes many relationships and marriages with it.

Personally, I found I could manage the business cash flow "sand timer of death" stress, as long as my personal life was in good shape. When there were problems at home, I found it extremely hard to simultaneously manage the spinning business plates of my start-up.

A supportive partner is like having a team of legends behind you. Remember, you are dragging them on this rollercoaster too and they may not have asked for it. People are often incredibly supportive and sympathetic in the early years, but over time, as you constantly inconvenience them with your choices (i.e., the business), the stress can wear away horribly at your personal life.

If the construction of every great building takes a life, the success of every great company can take a marriage. Do not let it be yours.

Even if the business goes bust, you will be back on your feet in a couple of years, with a new focus and great experience. If your relationship breaks up, it is highly likely to be gone forever.

In those early years, it may be possible for your partner to cover the essential household budget (mortgage, childcare, food, etc.). Particularly, while you get the business on its feet and can't afford to pay yourself a salary. This will transform your stress levels at work. Never, ever forget the sacrifice your partner and family are making on your behalf.

Confidence Is Key

You need to be **confident**. If you are not confident in yourself, your business, and your potential, why would anyone invest in you? Why would anyone else leave a stable job to work for you? I wouldn't. I am guessing you probably wouldn't either.

Become really good at **presenting the business**. Practice it repeatedly. Alone and in front of the team. It will give you confidence and build your resilience. It will help you visualize the company's future success and banish those butterflies of panic that will sometimes emerge in your stomach. Remember it is **all eyes on you**. In the early days, it is up to you to bring the bacon home with clients and investors.

A close friend asked me if I ever had any self-doubt, when I set up the company. I was shocked by the question. It never even occurred to me and you should be that way too, because believe me, on this journey, you are going to meet a **lot** of other people who will do that doubting on your behalf.

These will include failed entrepreneurs turned VCs, big company wage slaves "jealous" of your professional freedom, and investors who think your company is better off without you. Don't start to doubt yourself. If you do, you are finished.

Strategies for Staying Resilient

One of the big problems in setting up and growing a business, is that you need to be a **"big picture"** thinker, to have the vision and imagination to make it succeed. However, you also need to be a "small picture" thinker, to manage the detail and make it all happen. Very few people I have ever met are both. Most entrepreneurs don't enjoy working on the minutiae of day to day operations. It often really stresses them out. The way to solve this **"Entrepreneur Vision"** dilemma, is to hire primarily detail-oriented staff, who allow you to focus on the business strategy, while they tactically implement the company objectives.

Delegation is essential. Many entrepreneurs are terrible at it. It can be a learned skill. Hiring an intern or a couple of smart graduates is a great way to start handing over low level, but essential manual tasks, allowing you to focus on fundraising, product development and client acquisition. Handing over all accounting, corporate governance, and payroll duties to a good accountant can also free up hours of your time.

A large source of start-up stress comes from feeling hopelessly overwhelmed. You must build the right systems internally, to be able to take on more clients and more business, without drowning under the workload. That is why, it is important to **hire flexible staff**, who are keen to work on many aspects of the business and can grow in experience and rise in seniority, as the business expands.

Growing a great business is one massive collaboration. Don't forget that and treat everybody well, and you will have people coming out of the woodwork to help you during the hard times. When your largest prospect suddenly changes business strategy and you are not a part of it. When a key employee resigns from stress and goes to work for a competitor. Or when a global pandemic comes out of nowhere and threatens to destroy the business.

It can help to keep a **journal or diary** over these early years. Somewhere to document your thoughts and give you some perspective. It can help to decompress your thoughts and is a lot cheaper than therapy.

Find an outlet that you enjoy and helps you relax, and guard that time jealously. That could be running, playing a sport, or a musical instrument. For me, it was playing the drums and listening to The Beatles. For others, it could be drugs and narcotics. Do not go down that route. It will destroy you, your family, and your business.

One of the best ways to manage yourself through these difficult first few years, is to try and find someone who will act as an **entrepreneur coach**. There are not many around. Unfortunately, one of the shortcomings of modern coaching is that it tends to be focused on either personal wellness, or career and business advancement.

Life as an entrepreneur is not nicely sliced in two like this. What you need is an entrepreneur or a coach that can assist you in managing your personal life, while also providing the perspective you need, to help you think clearly about the business. Most business coaches are highly unlikely to have faced the monthly payroll firing squad. They have not experienced the stress or lived your pain.

This means the person you need to find as a mentor, should be an experienced entrepreneur. Someone who has done this before. Someone who understands the immense stress and workload involved in creating a new business. Someone who can offer meaningful insight into how best to square the circle of family and business life. An hour every week, or even fortnight, can transform your business outlook, and give you an outlet to discuss confidently all aspects of your life.

When investors say that every business should fill an unmet need, I have always felt the other unmet need it should fill is **within yourself.** I had worked in the same industry for two decades. It hadn't changed much. It was well paid but pretty boring. I knew it inside out and had a massive network across the world. If I had stayed doing the same work, I would have been bored to tears. Starting my own technology business became not so much "a nice to have," as it did a personal need.

Personally, I believe that if you have had lots of bad things happen to you in your own life, then you have a better chance of making it as an entrepreneur. This game is all about resilience and yours will be tested in a way very few people ever experience.

When I say bad things, I mean real tragedy. Family members younger than you dying. Divorce. Suicide. I do not mean parents passing away peacefully after eight decades of life.

If you have been able to pull your life back together from difficult events in your personal life, then you have a much better chance of having the resilience you need to make it through the years of start-up stress. You know how to survive.

If you have never experienced life shattering events, your reservoir of resilience is likely to be lower. The constant grind of financial, investor, client, and personal stress, will likely chew you up over those first few years.

Conclusion

It is called the "start-up grind" for a reason. Having a solid partner and family life, a personal well of resistance to draw upon, confidence in your business endeavors, and a positive attitude to see it through, will help massively.

Find an experienced entrepreneur to support and mentor you through the long days and the difficult nights.

Don't let the stress of managing the business turn you into a nasty person. It won't last forever. Develop the mental and emotional fortitude to pick yourself up each day and carry on regardless.

Chapter Summary

- Adopt strategies for dealing with personal and business stress.
- Learn to manage the four stakeholders in your life—family, employers, investors, and clients.
- Become greatly confident in what you are trying to achieve. If you believe in future success, it will make the down days easier.
- Delegate as much as possible to allow you to focus on the big picture and have a personal life.

- Find an outlet of personal enjoyment (e.g., music, sports, etc.) and guard it jealously.
- Find an ex-entrepreneur who can coach you and understands the stress you are under every day.
- Remember your personal life is a glass ball—if it falls, it will shatter forever.
- Your business life is a plastic ball—if its falls, it will not break. You can always get another job and will have bounced back in a couple of years.

CHAPTER 11

Managing Your Investors

Introduction

Think of finalizing your VC seed funding deal like a band signing a record contract. It's a great achievement, a real cause for celebration and an exciting milestone on the road to stardom. But guess what? Now you have to actually go and sell millions of records!

Now that you are a start-up funded by professional investors, you, as the CEO, have a whole new class of stakeholders to manage—your VC investors.

Managing investors, their expectations, timelines, reporting, and providing updates, as well as seeking new funding from Series A focused investors, is often a fulltime job for many start-up CEOs or near to it. You will have been shocked by the amount of time it took to find, agree, and finalize your seed funding deal. Now, your VC expects you to make good on your roadmap and projections, and deliver them the company growth you promised.

Great Investor Relations

Like every other relationship in life, the key to having a great relationship with your professional investors, is communication.

Good two-way communication breeds trust and this enables your VC to become another "trusted advisor" in your network. While the relationship is of course slightly different from other advisors, there is a huge amount you can learn from your VC. They have seen it all before. They have probably been in your shoes, having grown and sold businesses from nothing. They know the future mistakes you are going to make, often before you have even begun to think about your options.

The golden rule is that **a VC should never be just about the check.** There is so much more they can offer you; around mentoring, networking, operational advice, strategic guidance, tips on global expansion, and introducing warm business development leads.

Once your seed funding deal has closed, start putting in place the following:

1. **Monthly catch ups**—Update your VC regularly on your progress. At least on a monthly basis. Your seed funding deal will probably require quarterly Management Accounts to be provided to them (from your accountant). That's all well and good but it's nowhere near enough communication. Aim to have a monthly catch up with your key VC contact. Always prepare a list of "asks" for that conversation, including advice on strategy, hiring, who they might know at other VCs (for your next round) or at any prospective clients you are targeting.

2. **Seek operational advice**—Ideally your VC partner should be an ex-entrepreneur. These are the kind of investors you should be going with anyway and it can make a huge difference to your knowledge base. They will have lived your pain and would know every inch of "The Struggle."

   It is essential that you e-mail or call your VC informally every week (or as regular as you need to), in order to seek their guidance and operational input. The more formal strategic and commercial reviews can happen each month or at your company Board meetings.

   Ask them for operational advice on how to run and grow the business. Push them on this. They know your challenges coming up before you do. These discussions are not detailed commercial reviews but operational "touch bases" to pick their brains on where you are and what you are thinking of doing next. They will have valuable thoughts on how you can galvanize on potential opportunities and what pitfalls to avoid along the way.

   You will need advice on candidates to hire, markets to target next, key contacts in those locations, and in which company there might be the strongest prospect. Ask them what mistakes they are worried you might make soon, and what errors they made in the past. Push them hard for suggested contacts, as well as advice and support as the business expands. Having a great partnership with your VC can transform the business and is particularly valuable to you as the CEO.

3. **No nasty surprises**—You owe it to your VC to keep them abreast of any significant changes to the company. Every company has bad days. It's often not your fault. A large client changes strategy. Then you don't get picked for a big deal. A core employee leaves due to medical reasons and you have a massive hole to fill. There are many ups and downs on the way to greatness. It is best to be upfront and transparent about these matters to your investors. They can be surprisingly understanding and often have good ideas to help steady the ship.

4. **Marketing**—VCs can be a significant source of marketing for the business. You are an institutional funded start-up now, so trumpet it far and wide. Have your VCs issue a **separate press release** when your funding closes. Have them mention you in every press interview, blog post, or panel on which they speak. Having a professional investor sing your praises as a company regularly in the media, is far more valuable and credible than marketing from the company itself.

Similarly, when you are interviewed or publish articles and marketing collateral, make sure to mention what a great investment partner they are and how exciting it is to work together. Have them share your social media posts and marketing. Tag them in your LinkedIn and Twitter posts. **Constantly** remind the world you are VC funded. It will make client acquisition easier.

Always remember VCs are a vain bunch. They love to be praised. They love to feel that they have unearthed a diamond company in the rough. It makes them look prophetic and visionary. If you can praise them in a way that makes them proud, they will do everything they can to move your business forward.

5. **Future funding requirements**—Have early stage discussions with your VC on future funding requirements. These conversations should start within a few months of the seed round closing. Will you need a smaller "bridge round" (see the following) before your Series A to resource and close out a couple of impending client deals?

How much do they think you should raise for your Series A and at what Pre-Money Valuation? Who should you approach first, and can they help with the introduction? Your VC can be extremely helpful here and they will nearly always have significant contacts in their industry to help start early future funding discussions.

The Role of Bridge Funding

In the real world, the process from angel to seed to Series A is often choppy to say the least. Your carefully planned strategy can get torn to pieces if your funding round hits a legal snag or there is some other unforeseen delay. A bridge round is where you raise a small amount of money (often, but not always from your existing investor pool), to ensure you have enough operational capital to grow, while you close out your much larger Series A round.

I have closed a couple of bridging rounds over the years. They are normally quick and easy. They utilize the same seed round investment agreement (so the legal process is much reduced) and often the same pool of investors. They are rarely for more than a few hundred thousand dollars. Typically, the bridge round happens six to nine months after the seed round. This is when you are starting to bring in some decent revenue, but the costs of growing the business quickly is in danger of sucking any remaining seed funding dry.

For you as the CEO, a bridge round is a chance to revisit the company valuation. The first bridge round I did was seven months after the seed round. The company's valuation doubled for the bridge round, based on the progress we had made. This meant less dilution for the shareholders, and crucially, enabled us to market to Series A investors that we had **doubled our seed VCs investment (2x) in 7 months**. Series A VCs loved that.

It was a proven track record of fast value creation for a VC's investment portfolio. It made the Series A discussions much easier. It also injected a degree of urgency into the meetings because we had tangible evidence that the company's valuation was climbing quickly, and they needed to make an investment decision soon.

"Break Even" Revenue

While your focus as the CEO is to keep successfully scaling the business (and occasionally sleeping well at night), at some stage, you will soon start to think about the business reaching a "breakeven point" and finally having the incoming revenue needed to cover your costs. It is an attractive prospect after a couple of years living on the cliff edge.

Your VCs do not want to hear this. They want that famous "hockey stick" growth. Hockey stick growth means you will not reach breakeven for many years—if ever.

Many professional investors want you suckled on the milk of VC cash permanently. They do not want to hear about you being happy with reaching breakeven. This is for a number of reasons. They need a "home run" from you to make up for all their other investment losses. Also, they have far more control over you and your business if you constantly need scaling capital to keep growing. This in turn leads to faster increase in the value of their investment.

Preparing for Series A

You are always thinking about your next funding round—even before the current deal is closed.

As soon as your seed funding round is wrapped up, start thinking about your Series A. It will probably be a year away, but that time will pass quickly. How much do you think you will need? What will the valuation look like? What key milestones do you need to meet this year to get there?

Start to shortlist the VCs in your space that invest in Series A deals. Your seed VC will help you pull together a shortlist to focus on.

To start the Series A process, you need to leverage the investor relationships you have built up to date. **You don't pick up Series A funding from VCs you don't know**. At the multimillion investment level, that's not how it works.

Series A funding is heavily relationship based. You are about to go looking for at least a couple of million dollars to start scaling the business globally. This is real money. **Very** few companies get to this point. It is almost certainly the largest financial transaction you will ever have been involved in, never mind actually negotiated. The deal that emerges must allow you to spend these millions as you see fit, according to the scaling strategy you have devised.

Seed investors will not necessarily look at Series A rounds and vice versa. It depends on their investment strategy and investment mandate. This means you will need to build **new VC relationships** with the players that look at providing scaling capital. You probably won't have these contacts and you may be too busy running the company to build them. This is where your VCs network can be essential.

Your original VC (and even angel investors) can prove invaluable at this point. **Relentlessly mine their investor network.** If your seed VC agrees to come in again on your Series A (i.e., invest again at a higher valuation) that is a huge vote of confidence in you, your company, and your vision. Push them to do this. It will differentiate you from the pack of other seed funded start-ups, desperately trying to find scaling capital to grow and make raising a Series A that much easier.

Also, the **conversation with VCs changes** as you move closer to Series A. You are not discussing anymore how much you need to survive but instead how much funding you need to thrive. By now, you will start to have a track record of delivery as a CEO. If you are broadly executing your seed round growth strategy in accordance with your business plan and making good progress on client acquisition, then you are a much safer bet from a Series A VC perspective.

If you have closed a recent bridge round at a higher valuation, then broadcast far and wide the amazingly fast return on investment you made for your original VC.

Finally, ensure you have a **two-page Investment Summary** pdf ready to send immediately to interested investors. This summary is meant to whet their appetite and should be updated as and when you have new news to celebrate. It should include key wins, new client acquisitions, important hires, industry awards, press coverage, traction since your seed round, M&A approaches from interested buyers and a summary of the terms of your proposed Series A round (i.e., Pre-Money Valuation, funding being raised, expected closing date, etc.).

Conclusion

Great investor relations take time to cultivate and maintain. It is well worth it. The world of professional and VC investors is small, and they talk to each other constantly. A fast-growing start-up with a good reputation for open, transparent investor communication is at a significant advantage when they start looking for a Series A funding round from the market.

Chapter Summary

- Communication with your VC is key. Do it often and regularly.
- Monthly investor calls can be used for a more formal update.
- Regular operational catch ups can happen each week.
- Push your investors to help with company marketing.
- Consider a bridge funding round if its needed.
- Use your VC network to lay the foundations for your Series A funding round.
- Always have an up to date two-page Investment Summary available to send to potential investors.

CHAPTER 12

Selling to Large Companies

Introduction

As you become better known in your niche and have acquired a couple of initial respectable clients, word of the company and product will grow, and the large players will get to hear about you. After a time, they will want to check out your offering for themselves. This is the time to start engaging with them. They will have no interest in your solution before this point. You are just too small and fragile.

There are two primary ways to land a large client:

- "Land and Expand"
- Winning a Request for Proposal ("RFP")

RFPs are formal tender documents large companies use when they are looking for a new service. They are a pain and take a long time to complete.

"Land and Expand" is where you begin a small project for one team or location in a large organization. They are far easier and less soul destroying.

We will look at both in detail next.

Once you get seed funded and you start targeting the big boys in the industry, the thing that will **kill** your growing technology business is not the delays with funding, the endless juggling of cash flow, or the pain of trying to hire the best talent with no resources; it is the **Slow No**.

Remember that phrase. It haunts the dreams (and mainly nightmares) of many failed entrepreneurs.

The "slow no" is the long procurement cycle of most large companies. It is being passed endlessly from team to team, from IT to the procurement department and back to the operation teams once again, without ever getting a clear yes or no from anyone. It will take up months of company time and if not managed carefully can destroy your business.

Ignore the fancy PR from big companies about their fast innovation and partnerships with small innovative companies. The "no one was ever fired for hiring IBM" mentality still applies at most large organizations. Big companies are normally very conservative and slow to adopt new innovation. Their typical buying process can be from one to three years. It is extremely easy to get stuck indefinitely in this hamster wheel of indecision.

If your product is real, new groundbreaking technology that will change their business, you will **face a second problem**. You are going to have to **educate** them about this new technology and its huge benefits to their organization. You can get stuck working with their innovation labs for years, with nothing to show for it except a paid "Proof of Concept" product trial and with very little chance, they will put the solution into their "production" (i.e., live) work environment anytime soon.

Just like with your investors, to bring in a huge global company, you need to build up a **great relationship** over many months (often at least a year), while simultaneously working out a **palatable commercial deal** that they can digest internally.

Many of these organizations have strict rules about working with software vendors that have less than $10 million on their balance sheet and at least eighteen months runway in contractual revenue on their books. To get around these nominal roadblocks, you need to be clever and often start the relationship with a small, focused project (e.g., $50,000 to $100,000).

That is why it is key to sign up those couple of reputable, fast growing mid-tier firms in the industry, **before** going after the big guys. The references from these clients are invaluable at enabling you to jump some of these later hurdles. The big companies watch closely what the hungry, smaller players do. If they are at conferences or watching online marketing videos, where the competition they fear is raving about your product, you will find it much easier to open their door.

Selling Process to Big Global Businesses

I have the typical entrepreneur personality. This supposedly means I am predisposed to social encounters and energized by dealing with a wide circle of people. While this is basically true, nothing prepared me for the circle of relationships I would have to manage successfully, when trying to deploy our software at some of the largest global financial players.

You are dealing with **at least three** internal groups:

1. **The internal sponsor**—That is, the manager from the business itself, who is screaming for your product and wants it now.
2. **The procurement team**—Their whole job is to beat down the commercial deal you just spent nine months agreeing with your internal sponsor.
3. **The technology team**—The company's internal IT department who often want nothing to do with you and are incredibly adept at making themselves unavailable to you for technology reviews. You are probably a threat to them. If your software is as revolutionary as you say it is, that's even worse. Then you are even more of a threat to them.

Remember, for the Procurement team and the IT team, there is **no upside** to working with you.

That's exactly why Intrapreneurs (what a joke!) at large companies don't work. There is no real upside if things go right, but plenty of downside, if things go wrong.

How to Manage Objections

While you certainly didn't set up the business to get into a form of "marriage guidance," that is what you are about to have to do. Let's be honest here. Most of these people at huge companies don't know, never mind like, each other. Large, global organizations are the size of small cities. A staff of 100,000 is not that uncommon.

You need to find out who is the real buyer. **Who controls the budget** and who can write the check? In a gigantic organization, that is more difficult than it seems.

Longer term, when you are in the door and exploring long-term expansion and innovation plans with this keystone client, the secret becomes finding out **who makes the budget**.

Working With the Internal Sponsor

The internal sponsor is the person at the big company who loves your product and will champion the solution internally. You will need to work hard to foster a great, collaborative relationship with this person. That means drinks, dinners, travelling to business events to see them speak; all the usual requirements to build up a solid, long-term business relationship.

The initial deal will have to work to their budgetary requirements, and you should not let this first step be railroaded by your rate card. It is important to be flexible and evolve a genuine collaborative business partnership. A deep relationship will serve you well, when (not if) road bumps in the implementation project appear later on.

Quite frankly, you need to have the business sponsor in your back pocket. If you don't, your exciting initiative will be lost in the fog of higher priorities, new crisis, and changes in strategy from senior management.

Managing the Procurement Team

The job of the procurement team is to get the best deal possible for the client.

They can be very painful for you and a complete roadblock to the project moving forward.

Put yourself in their mindset. They have nothing whatsoever to gain from the successful implementation of your product.

This means you need to negotiate carefully and structure the deal, so it looks like good value to them. Give them something that doesn't cost you anything to sweeten the deal (additional training, some consulting, etc.). Perhaps tell them that you used to buy software before and know what unreliable vendors can be like.

Tell them explicitly you are happy to put in the contract that there will be no hidden charges whatsoever. Acknowledge that many software companies are notorious for this (like a drug dealer scam of getting the kids hooked cheap and then jacking up the price), and as demonstrated evidence that this is **not** your business model; agree that all additional fees and expenses outside of the contract have to be agreed and signed off by the client in advance. These can sometimes include random customizations they may request, a new report they want to build or travel to a far-flung regional office.

This can help put out the fires somewhat and take down the temperature of the negotiations.

Make the point to them, that unlike most vendors, you offer full and complete support over year ends, key holidays, and quarter ends. You will have to look at providing this. Many other small technology companies can only provide extended U.S. or European business hour coverage (i.e., 8 am–7 pm local time). That does not cut it for global organizations in the modern business world.

Ironically, key large company dates are often over business holidays (e.g., December 31st in the U.S./Europe and June 30th in Australia). I have seen technology business relationships get into serious trouble because the client had no one to call at 9 pm on a quarter end, when they were experiencing real technical difficulty. It is awfully hard to come back from that kind of disaster. Don't let it happen to you.

Tell the procurement team that you will release updates every quarter and only seek to deploy it after written approval for evening or weekend access (if required). Any bugs will be reviewed and corrected when they give prior approval. You will not have any access to their private server or data unless it is provided by them for routine or requested maintenance.

Most easy of all, ask them for **their** standard vendor contract and try to make it **global**. It is much easier and faster that way. New offices can be brought onto the platform much faster in the future. The procurement team won't even glance at the contract you used with your first client. The game has changed now. You are competing and delivering with the big boys and it has to be done on their terms, or you will go nowhere.

Be aware that many big companies now centralize their investment and purchasing decisions in their global headquarters. That means that the real money—the mid-six figure and above deals—are only able to be approved and signed off at these locations (e.g., New York City or in London). That is where the procurement team will also be based. These guys don't know who you are. Moreover, they don't care *("You want to spend HOW MUCH with this tiny software company we have never heard of?").*

For us, being in Ireland, it was a problem. Local office approval for a project up to $100,000 was possible, but anything above that threshold normally had to be reviewed in detail and signed off by the procurement team. That team was inevitably based at the company's global headquarters. For us that meant London, which thankfully was easily accessible. For you, it may not be that easy to get in front of the procurement manager. Their green light is essential to get the deal over the line.

The "Land and Expand" Strategy

Most large global businesses agree to new technology budgets on an annual basis and they mostly kick into place each January. Pulling this together normally begins the previous September or October. If your product is not included in that budget for January, it makes it extremely hard to get approval for a large technology deal outside of that annual expenditure cycle.

However, many departments and teams often have a smaller, local expense budget. This can be spent on ad-hoc improvements and smaller technology projects.

One way of procuring a large client is to get your product in the door initially under a small engagement. That way, it can potentially bypass the strict global company procurement process.

This model is known as "land and expand." It involves finding a business sponsor for the solution and agreeing an initial smaller deal with them, under their own budgetary approval. This might be an initial $50,000 or $100,000 to try out the product within their department and test it for value and usability.

Once they have used the solution for a few months and are convinced of its merits, it is much easier to have it approved internally for a wider project roll out across the company. This process takes time, but is a useful incremental way to build a business relationship that is sticky and can be extremely profitable long term, once you perform as they expect.

With these large companies, it is all about de-risking the purchase process for them. The fact that you have a proven track record internally and have demonstrated that you are a reliable vendor is a huge step on the way to companywide implementation.

Set up your rate card so that the initial cost of the product fits within a smaller operating budget, while having significant potential upside as the solution is rolled out across the world.

This model allows you to ramp up internally on a gradual basis. It also gets around many of the "but this is a small company with a tiny balance sheet" objections that the procurement teams at large companies use to scupper start-up technology vendors.

Managing an RFP

Sometimes, there's just no way around completing an RFP. This is a formal "Request for Proposal" issued by a large company, when they want to buy a new product or service.

Completing RFPs can be a good learning experience for your team, as you learn to understand and expect the key questions and level of detail, large companies require before they will even consider using the product.

Choose your RFPs wisely. You can't possibly respond to each one. Completing an RFP properly can take at least a week. And most of these contracts, you will not win.

Set up an **RTP database** of questions you will always be asked (e.g., company history, investors, current clients, financials, etc.) and populate it gradually over time with good detailed answers to all the questions you are asked. Put them in different buckets (e.g., operations, legal, risk management, technology architecture, etc.) and add to them with each new tender.

Annoyingly, we found that each RFP was slightly different and the same area (e.g., procurement, technology) would often ask a variation on the questions we had answered in the previous tenders. There is no real way to avoid this. It's a pain and all technology companies hate the RFP process.

It is far better to be **invited** into an RFP by a company you already know. Perhaps you have already met them and had coffee with them. Even better if they have already seen your product informally and know a bit about the business. Having some sort of existing relationship makes it much easier to find out what works for them commercially and what the key metrics are, that they need from you to make the contract work.

For large companies:

- Short term—Find out who can **approve spending from the budget**
- Long term—Find out who **makes the budget.** These are senior managers that can write the big checks.

The smaller players you have implemented to date do not have gigantic risk management and mitigation policies in place. They won't have had dozens of data management and technology integration policies that must be adhered to. Your large new client will, and you will be expected to strictly comply with them.

It's important that the commercials you agree to recognize the work involved in the implementation process. You may have charged anywhere between $10,000 and $50,000 to implement the solution at the first couple of smaller clients. For this first large player, you need to **charge a substantial onboarding fee**; certainly, well over $100,000. Otherwise, the economics just won't work. You will need to hire new client relationship, technology, and development staff, to ensure a large client is properly serviced and resourced.

Managing Large Company Integrations

Once you agree to a big deal with a large company, it becomes a complicated process of managing existing clients, while simultaneously ramping up for your first large integration.

Managing a large global onboarding, when you're only a small company, is a delicate balancing act. This means breaking down the client's requirements, their locations, initial teams, key deliverables, and expected "ramp up" onto your solution and working out how best to deliver it.

Work with the project sponsor to agree on a realistic "**Onboarding Plan.**" That should spell out in detail the initial deliverables expected from you in phase one and the timeline around it. The client also needs to commit a project team or internal resources on their side to work with you closely on delivery.

In a large company, that can be more complicated than it seems. Many of their project teams will have fulltime day jobs, meaning they are probably terribly busy and not especially motivated by the extra work of onboarding your wonderful solution or the disruption it will bring to their lives. If they have specific resources to **allocate fulltime** to the product integration, then that is fantastic.

The first key item that needs to be agreed is the **joint "Onboarding Plan."** Get ahead of the client on this. As soon as your team has finished celebrating winning the deal and your head is clear, draft a first version "for discussion" and send it to them immediately.

Use your original Implementation Plan as the template for this project. It will be too high level for a huge global project but the key areas (e.g., set up, training, testing, data import, etc.) will be the same and it's a good starting point. Use the **information gained in the RFP** to begin expanding it substantially. This will make you look both proactive and professional. It is exactly how a game-changing relationship like this should kick off.

From earlier discussions with the client, or from the RFP they provided, you will have an outline understanding of how they want to onboard. It may be one office location at a time (or even one team). They may then want to expand globally, once that first location is bedded in. They may even decide they want to be more conservative and have their project team **test** your solution extensively, before then deciding to put it live in their real business environment.

A large onboarding project **typically takes months and often a number of quarters**. That works better for you, because it gives you more time to resource properly and address any teething problems that arise. Having won this deal, you will be playing catch up to expand the team quickly in order to service the contract. Having more time works in your favor.

Ideally, for a large client, the **first quarter should be spent setting up the solution** for them internally. This would include extensively training the first users, documenting how they intend to use your solution, importing any data and initial documentation for set up and then conducting extensive user testing in their test environment.

Having these first few months enables a number of **dry runs** of the software in their world. It also enables you to become extremely familiar with their internal processes. This is essential. You will have some idea from the RFP discussions, but a whole lot will emerge in the setup phase, that won't have been discussed previously. New requirements, presumptions (by them), service demands, and particularly, data management and risk issues, all appear when they are spending real money with you.

Quarter two would then be spent on ramping up the rollout across the first office and beyond the initial project team. Training more internal users, addressing any teething issues and really bedding down the solution at your client internally. This will involve extensive relationship management, documenting any new business processes and agreeing a set of further technology functionality, they will likely request from the product.

While an onboarding process like this would be the ideal situation, with large companies, you are **dancing to their tune** and they will call the shots on the integration timeline they want. If it's much too fast for you, all you can do is seek to counsel them from a risk management perspective and suggesting a more conservative onboarding schedule would be prudent. You can't push back too hard at this stage; in case they get cold feet on the whole project. They are probably already out on a limb just by choosing your solution.

Your whole team must be laser focused on managing this integration. As the CEO, you need to appoint a dedicated project manager for the client integration. Not a relationship management or business development resource. An **experienced software implementation manager** who understands the steps involved in managing complex global rollouts and can anticipate and solve onboarding issues before and as they arise.

Build your own internal team to face the client and make sure, at the very least, it includes a project manager, an experienced technical developer, your product manager, the relevant client relationship person and a junior technical member of the team, to manage data and initial user testing.

As the CEO, you will have to be part of this integration team too. Ideally, you could leave the project manager to run things, but it is just too important for the future of the company that the project is a success. You will have to be heavily involved.

Depending on the resources, you may even need to be the dedicated project manager on this first big implementation. Once your team has done a few of these projects, then you don't need to be involved day to day. Instead you can attend the weekly and fortnightly joint project meetings with the client.

First time around, however, it's all hands-on deck. That means you. If the project goes badly and the client pulls the plug, you can forget about a Series A funding deal. It is extremely hard to come back from a setback like that.

The Role of Implementation Partners

One option to manage a project of this size, is to choose an **implementation partner**. In this model, your team manages the technology and your partner works globally, at the client's various locations, to manage the onboarding and roll out. The large advisory and professional service companies are always keen to partner with technology vendors on projects of this size.

However, it is **not recommended** to use a partner like this for the **first** big client onboarding. It is important for the team to learn how to do this themselves. You need to build up the internal knowledge base for managing these large global integrations. The ups and downs of the project will be a steep learning curve for your relatively inexperienced team, but it is nearly always the best way to learn.

You can consider an implementation partner for future enterprise level projects. This could happen because another new client demands that you send ten people to their Hong Kong office for three months to manage the rollout. If there are only 12 people in the company, this represents a big problem. Having the right local implementation partners can alleviate this problem.

Conclusion

The reason you are busy scaling the company globally, is to be able to get to the point where the business can seamlessly manage these types of large projects. This is where the big money comes from. The adoption of your software by many new offices will add massively to the bottom line, materially impact the next investment valuation, and can give you clients in every corner of the globe. At that point, your business is no longer valued in millions, but in tens of millions.

Chapter Summary

- Manage all three core relationships at your first large client carefully—Business Sponsor, Procurement department & Client IT team.
- Deal with their objections one by one.
- Structure the deal with plenty of upside as use of the solution expands globally.
- Charge the large client a hefty implementation fee to cover the huge cost in both acquiring and onboarding them.
- Produce a draft Onboarding Plan immediately on winning the deal.
- Push for a multiquarter implementation.
- Consider an implementation partner for future large global integrations.

CHAPTER 13

Scaling the Company Globally

Introduction

If you don't go global, you will only ever be local.

Investors won't want to fund you unless you target global expansion.

Even if investors want to fund you and government agencies want to back you, leading global companies in your industry won't work with you—and why would they, when you can't support them globally.

The time to think about scaling internationally is when you close your seed round.

How you scale and when you do it is critically important to driving company valuation and setting yourself up for the second round of clients. The biggest potential clients in your niche operate in every major time zone and have important staff resources spread all around the major global business centers. And you will be expected to be able to support them if they make the decision to purchase your product.

You will need to find the right people, sign the right partnerships, and attract the right advisors, to be able to take the business global.

In Ireland, when new start-up entrepreneurs would tell me they were planning to go global quickly, I always asked them the same question—What U.S. Business Visa have you applied for?

Perhaps your local government or even other technology companies will help you expand overseas. We had assistance like this in London, New York, and Australia. It made a huge difference and we learned a massive amount about the local business market in each jurisdiction. You can do the same. Just don't forget to praise all the help you receive in every media interview you give afterwards.

Where to Scale?

If you know your industry well, it will be obvious where you should expand to next. If you are in FinTech, that could be London. If you are in MedTech, it might be Switzerland, and if you are selling software to manage oil refineries, maybe that would be Texas.

The key point is to have a strategy in place that will eventually cover **all three major time zones**. That is, a presence in The Americas, a base in Europe (to also cover the Middle East and Africa) and a footprint in Asia-Pacific to manage any client acquired there.

Having this stated in your growth strategy early will impress investors. Executing on a well thought out scaling strategy significantly **enhances your business valuation**. It will also be essential if you want to bring home a huge business titan from your industry. The whales of every market tend to have multiple offices and tens of thousands of people globally. Without a realistic plan for how you will support them, you won't get past the first demo.

By starting to scale **before** you have secured a Series A funding round, you will signify to the market and potential VC investors that you are serious about becoming a global technology company; and you are embarking on this expansion strategy, regardless of whether they are involved or not.

You will only have the funding to take baby steps globally, but it will impress investors and differentiate your business from the other seed technology companies that "talk the talk" about worldwide expansion.

Choosing where to scale into is an exciting process. It will happen as you are targeting more clients locally too, so as always with start-ups, it becomes a balancing act for the team and especially your own time.

There are different ways you can start to build an overseas presence. Many entrepreneurs would suggest an experienced local salesperson as a great first step. The problem is you will not have any money to pay them.

The Challenge of Scaling Successful

The important point is this. **A CEO will have to spend significant time in any target overseas market.** You won't have the funds to recruit much of a team locally, so you will have to do it yourself. This means, you will have to spend a huge amount of time pounding the pavements abroad. We spent weeks and weeks in New York. We had umpteen strong NYC coffees a day. I was in Australia for long periods too. The company still needed to be run while I was away.

After you draw down your seed funding check (probably an amount somewhere between $500,000 and $1 million), you are feeling on top of the world and huge vistas of possibilities open up for you and your team. The world really does feel like it could be your oyster. Hold onto that feeling. You are going to need it.

Even though you can't be everywhere at once, over the next year, you are going to have to try to be. Prepare yourself for a huge amount of travel. Living in cheap hotels (we even used hostels), grabbing a quick sandwich on the go, and never eating a home cooked meal for weeks on end.

There is no real way around this. You need to get your family and partner onboard. You also need to ensure you have enough of a team in place to run things day-to-day, while you are abroad. In reality, at this stage of development, you also need to keep your eye actively involved on what's happening back at company HQ. This is an exceedingly difficult task.

When you target a new market as a small company, people expect to meet the CEO. They don't want to meet some new member of staff from a company they have never heard of. Later, in the expansion, you can leave a trusted business development resource behind to move things forward and/or give that role to a local advisor who has helped start the ball rolling.

I often spent a full day in New York having six meetings, coffees, and demos, and then in the evening catching up on home business. Putting out fires, dealing with client queries, and answering a multitude of staff questions. Your home team will still be pretty new and when you are on the road for weeks on end, they need daily calls to discuss critical issues and for you to provide suitable guidance.

In the first scaling year of business, I wished for nothing else than to be able to clone myself. The same thing will happen to you. The problem with scaling at this point in your business story is that it's utterly exhausting.

However, for my company, there really was no other choice. The total cost of hiring a top class FinTech salesperson in New York, with a great network, and a proven track record, was around $250,000. A couple of them and that's your seed round spent. And don't forget they may be rubbish. They may not perform and then your business is dead in the water.

I rapidly concluded that I would have to drive the New York expansion myself. There was no other choice.

Alternatively, you can appoint a (free, at this stage) **advisor in your targeted market**, in lieu of future remuneration and/or "sweat equity." We also did this, and it worked well. It meant immediate access to their local business network and credibility when we came to pitch.

You can evolve your advisors gradually into salespeople if you have a good relationship. They can start on a commission basis or a small retainer, and then they can be brought into a more permanent role as you expand. We found most of our advisors through friends of friends and on LinkedIn. Any of these advisors who also wanted to help us with sales, were paid a percentage of the core license fee, for the first two years of each deal they brought onboard.

Creating Awareness Quickly in a New Market

Your **government start-up body** may be able to help with finding, or even providing, cheap local office space. Go to the start-up hubs in your target city, look at the shared office space, and even speak to your embassy or consulate in town. They can be a surprisingly great source of contacts, leads, and a desk for a few weeks, while you find your feet.

Buy a cheap Skype phone number in your target city. You can find one for less than ten dollars a month online. Redirect it to your personal mobile phone. Put the overseas number on your business cards, website, and marketing documentation. Now, you have a **local business number** in your desired overseas location, and it will appear that you have an office there too.

When I had a consultancy in London, I moved back to Ireland. But I bought a local London number off Skype and it rang my cell phone at home. Similarly, when we targeted both New York and Australia, we bought local Manhattan and Sydney numbers online. We had them printed on our business cards, and all of a sudden, we had a presence in every major time zone (Americas, EMEA, and APAC). We were a global business.

When you start to spend time in your target city, set up a **local "Meetup"** group covering your area of interest. Invite everyone in your LinkedIn network locally to join the group. Keep its tone neutral and not sales focused. For example, "The NYC Blockchain group," "The London Insurance Technology Meetup." Add to the group name as "Powered by Company XYZ." Just like you did when you set up your LinkedIn group.

Then, once you have a few hundred members, **set up a local "Meetup" event**, discussing the "key trends and future opportunities" in the market. This will cost some money for beers and light snacks, but you may be able to wing the venue space for free (perhaps the main start-ups' hubs).

Invite **three or four local heroes** in your industry to sit on the panel and you as the CEO appear as well. Have one of your team, who presents well, be the event moderator. Film the whole event. Make up a number of short videos to share each week on social media and interview the audience at the event (hopefully, saying how great it was and how insightful). Ensure that behind your panel, you have the company logo emblazoned onscreen or on a banner. These events can be a great way to get quick recognition in a target market.

We did two industry Meetup events in NYC and the total cost was $1,000 each (and that was for the beers and some food). Companies can be surprisingly generous with their corporate space, if one of them can appear on the panel.

Write pieces on the company expansion and publish them on LinkedIn, Medium, and back home in relevant industry and technology publications. Many technology websites are keen to publish news on local start-ups expanding abroad. It is a great news story.

This is all building awareness of the business and driving its valuation. The industry will get to know you and investors will see you are delivering on a global rollout and you are hungry with ambition.

Researching an Overseas Market Properly

Before deciding where to scale, **research** the market thoroughly. We were targeting fund managers in the United States, just like we had done in the UK. In the European Market, a $5 billion market was a decent medium sized fund manager. In the United States, they were a tiny minnow. In Europe, the same manager would have had a team of seventy compliance staff for us to sell our software to. In the United States, there would be a dozen people in the company and one guy would do the compliance part-time.

We had to radically update our U.S. business development strategy, as well as our marketing collateral and pricing model. We came to realize that the size of the fund manager we needed to target in New York, was managing $25 to $50 billion dollars, a gigantic sum of money in Europe. A company this size was not easy to get into, so we had a dual focused strategy. Finding a local partner and massively increasing my number of LinkedIn connections.

We bought a cheap database of all the fund managers in the United States—the size of the funds, key contacts, and assets under management. When we landed to start the local push, we had already arranged a dozen demos with small and medium fund managers in New York City.

LinkedIn was a major driver to putting these local meetings in place. As a recognized thought leader in your industry, it's so much easier to add anyone on LinkedIn and have them to connect with you. Ever since I wrote a book on hedge funds in 2012, I found it super easy to grow my professional network globally. People see "author" and they think they better be connected to this guy.

We had to be shrewd in how we grew our New York connections. I already had a couple of hundred contacts, but we wanted to get to well over a thousand relevant staff at fund managers in the area. We then needed to message many of them directly and ask to see them, either for a meeting or at least a coffee.

To do this, and not seem like just another sales hack, we added all the relevant people we could find in New York on LinkedIn and then waited three or four weeks. It was only then we sent each one of them individually (painful but necessary) a direct message on LinkedIn. As it was from someone they were already connected with, and not sales orientated, we received over a 75 percent response rate.

The template e-mail I drafted was changed each time adding in the person's name. We also made the message look like an individually crafted e-mail every time. This asked how the weather was in New York and that you hoped all was good at XYZ company. We explained that we were an Irish FinTech opening a new office in New York and were keen to meet some of the leading players locally. We would love to buy them a coffee to learn a bit more about the key trends taking place in the New York funds industry and we could share a few insights too, from what was happening over here in Europe.

Some of the best connections I have made over the course of a 25-year career came from that one message.

In New York, anyone will meet you for a 20-minute coffee. We used to tell them we were new in town and wanted to get the "lie of the NYC land," and we would provide the same for them "from across the pond." This worked every time. People always met us, as long as we were polite and not too sales oriented.

Also, in New York, they will tell you within 15 minutes whether or not they are interested. That the product is not for them, but they know someone who might be interested. That's the great thing about New York— "everyone knows someone."

Try and scale **on the back of other successful technology companies** from your hometown or country. They can often be happy to help you. You can return the favor to other startups when you are successful. We were greatly assisted by other Irish companies that had successfully cracked the U.S. market. We had offers of office space, joint industry, and drinks events, and even the free use of technical developers. Every country has a diaspora. Mine yours.

Publish widely the companies global expansion, as a "how to" guide for other companies. We published a series of articles in the main Irish technology news website, about opening in the United States and the ups and downs we experienced. Honest accounts and "war stories" covering everything from how to find apartments, to office space, to opening a bank account, and getting that first U.S. client over the line.

You may have to give another "sweetheart" deal to the first client at your overseas location. It will likely be a small contract the first time around. No one knows you and they are not going to take a big chance.

Ideally, you will not have to give anyone a free trial of your software but quite frankly, you may end up doing just that. That way you can get their feedback, understand any new product requirements for the local market and be able to trumpet in company marketing that you "have companies in New York using our solution."

Once you have one client in a new market, things get much easier. Having a reference to provide from a local company brings local credibility. We found that particularly in some Asia-Pacific markets like Australia. One of the first questions we were often asked was "who else are you working with locally."

Why Massive Failure Can Be Acceptable

Learn to accept when scaling abroad, that massive failure is ok. It takes up to seventy meetings to find a good, profitable business client. After five years, our CRM told me we had conducted about five hundred sales related meetings. Some of these were coffees, most were demos, some were workshops, and we had had multiple meetings with many companies.

At that point, we had perhaps a dozen clients. That means we had a **98 percent business development failure rate.** The key takeaway here is that a **two percent success rate works** fine for a B2B business development strategy. Less than a dozen clients were enough for us to receive a Series A Term Sheet.

This was because we had shown we had product market fit, we had a mix of small and medium clients across the world and we were growing the business internationally.

Conclusion

As you expand abroad, you will start to be approached by interested third parties. Some will want to buy you (most likely), some will want to partner, and some may just want to copy and steal your product. Tread carefully. Big companies are notorious for doing this. You need to ensure you don't take your scaling eye off product innovation. Keep the company's product and strategy one step ahead of the competition.

Now is the time to start thinking about your Series A funding round. The seed round will be six to twelve months behind you, you will have a couple more client wins and a couple of bigger fish in the pipeline. The first tentative steps into overseas expansion will crystallize the funding and resources you will need to scale properly internationally. Use these insights to fully inform the amount of Series A funding you will need to raise.

Chapter Summary

- Your first international location should be the global center of your industry.
- Find a local business advisor you trust, to help with introductions and scaling challenges.
- Begin researching and contacting peers in the local market a few months before you land.
- Use Meetups and local industry events as a great way to meet potential clients and create company awareness quickly.
- Host your own company event covering the major trends taking place in your industry.
- Expect to have to offer a "sweetheart" deal to your first international client.
- The "Land and Expand" model of client acquisition works well in a new market where you are unknown.
- If you acquire at least two percent of the business customers you meet, you can still be successful.
- Taking the first steps internationally adds significantly to the company valuation.
- Consider local partners to help implement your solution on the ground.
- To capitalize on your initial global expansion, you will need to build a proper team. That is why you need the Series A funding round.

CHAPTER 14

Innovating for Growth

Introduction

You already know the importance of innovation. It was the reason you set up the business in the first place. Innovating constantly will enable you to become a market leader within your chosen business niche.

You are still nimble, you can still be quick. You can innovate, expand, launch, and implement new and existing products quickly. Then deploy them in the market to clients within weeks (not months or years like larger software vendors).

For many investors and prospective clients, ongoing technology innovation is often considered a leading indicator of future financial success. If you have an interesting first product and you have a well thought out roadmap for further innovation, it is much easier to get them to fund or partner with your business.

After your seed funding round and for the first time since you began this journey, you may have some cash. Probably not much but enough to give you some product development options. Target at least **20 percent** of your cash for innovation, R&D, and new development.

Twenty percent may sound a lot but it's a requirement if you are to stay ahead of the pack. Post seed round is the time for you to hire a dedicated product manager. This will be someone with the experience and vision to create and manage the company's "Product Roadmap," for which you will provide oversight, guidance, and validation. It is having someone on board to think about product innovation fulltime and work with the development team to manage its delivery.

Now that the company is seed funded, you need to refocus on innovation for two reasons:

- It is a major driver of **revenue**.
- It is a major driver of **future company valuation**.

Innovation for Revenue Growth

As an exciting, new start-up, your game-changing technology will be the primary reason the first real client signed up to use your solution.

You need to leverage that relationship to drive future revenue growth. From the earliest period of implementation, the first client will have requested enhancements and made suggestions for additional functionality. Subsequent clients will be the same. Some of these requests will be amazing ideas and some will be irrelevant.

Ask your clients for their input and guidance into your Product Roadmap. It's an invaluable source of market research, as it is straight from the coal face. Also, as you, as an entrepreneur, become more immersed in scaling your business, you will move away from being an SME in your space and more an expert on how to grow a technology business. You won't be involved in the day-to-day of your industry as much anymore.

That is why the real-world view of your clients can be invaluable. It enables you to validate what your tech and product guys are proposing for your solution and whether there is an immediate market for any new development.

Our technology was used in many ways we never suspected by our initial clients, once they went live. We had built a solution for monitoring their compliance. They started to use it for managing product launches. Internal audit teams began utilizing the data and then enhancing the reporting. Teams that were focused on risk and operations started using the software to manage operational due diligence. We had thought of precisely none of these ways to use the software.

All of these new use cases for the technology made sense. They expanded the footprint at our initial clients, both at the kick-off location and then when they expanded globally. It made the clients far stickier and ramped up our revenue nicely.

Client Sponsoring Innovation

To meet new customers use cases, you will need to expand the technology and functionality in the product. Through financial necessity you may not have the funds or revenue at this point to deliver these enhancements.

The trick here is to **make clients pay for these new developments.** They can then be sold across the market.

To do this, you need to get clients on board to pay for new development. When you update key customers at their quarterly catch up, ask for their feedback on the current Product Roadmap. Offer to fast track any particular items they are especially interested in. For this, you need to ask them to "sponsor" that development.

This means they are the first to have this new functionality. They can guide its development, provide substantial input into the requirements, and ensure what is delivered is completely "fit for purpose" for them internally.

You and your product manager will have to ensure that what you build is fit for the wider market and not just for that client. This takes judgment, research, understanding your broader markets requirements, and the ability to push back appropriately, when you believe your sponsoring clients' needs are not aligned with the market's future demand.

It is important to give these product innovation discussions a sense of urgency. Tell them you are going to ask all your clients if they want to sponsor the proposed developments but as your flagship client, you wanted to offer them the first right of refusal. However, they need to let you know by the end of next week.

Price the new development so that it minimizes the possibility of internal pushback. Many teams have innovation budgets and can approve a development quickly if it stays within a five-figure cost. Ask for one third up front. One third on development delivery and one third on full deployment. This minimizes their financial pain and covers your technology costs for the development.

Vendors are often asked by new or existing clients whether they have some new unheard of or unthought of piece of functionality. Their standard answer is "it's on our roadmap." This is the software vendors equivalent of "it's in the post"!

The **difference** here is that you and your product manager will have thought carefully about what needs to go into the roadmap and that you will be able to talk in detail about all the aspects of these requirements, regulatory, compliance, and risk factors.

Innovation for Valuation Growth

Innovation is key to driving company valuation, while also staying attractive to investors and at the forefront of any industry.

Every exciting technology business should have a **secret sauce** that drives it. This, along with the team, is what investors are interested in owning a slice of.

It is a major driver of business valuation, especially as it starts to be adopted in the industry and it begins to look like the skies are the limit.

The key message is this:

- **Start-ups that have a "secret sauce" enjoy a higher valuation**. Often **much higher**. Investors and prospective clients will put you in the bucket of "game-changing" innovation.
- **Start-ups with no secret sauce will achieve a lower valuation**. Often **much lower.** Particularly if your product seems like it can be easily "commoditized" by new entrants into the industry.

We knew one technology company in an emerging FinTech space. They went out to raise a Series A (circa $2 million dollars) at a valuation of $12 million. However, because they were considered to have some cutting edge innovation, and some pretty good run rate revenue lined up over the following year ($2 million), as well as building a good name in the conference circuit—they ended up raising $8 million at a valuation of $40 million.

This kind of funding is available. It can be you who brings it home. You just need to have a growth story in place for investors. This means your "secret sauce" is embedded in the product, with plenty of upside to come.

Constantly innovating as you scale the business will keep and enhance your Secret Sauce. It will also place you at the forefront of the industry and a market leader on new trends and technology.

To investors, you must be able to demonstrate that you have thought diligently and strategically about what your industry is going to need in the future and how you plan to deliver it. Future industry and client requirements need to feature firmly on the Product Roadmap.

Key to doing this, as you scale, is publishing regular and highly regarded **thought leadership** pieces on new industry trends. Do not underestimate the impact on company valuation from a constant, regular stream of well-regarded industry thought pieces. These articles are about informing your audience and not marketing to them. They should be educational in tone and never used as a form of business development.

Articles like these should focus on the "current trends and future opportunities" in the industry. The current trends are straightforward; they are plain for all to see. What matters is your take on them and how you believe they will extrapolate and impact the industry in the future.

For example, a piece could be called "5 key trends in aviation AI" or "New trends in documentary filming technology." The important thing is to indirectly outline how they relate to your business and how your solution will address these new trends.

Being able to share interesting thought leadership pieces (see more in Chapter 5 on Marketing) to both investors and prospective clients, is enormously powerful for your brand. It is also key to getting big players to buy the product. If your thought leadership pieces fill an educational role, then they are valuable to your client base.

Acquisition Interest

By the time of your Series A funding round, you will start to be approached by interested third parties. Some will want to partner with you, some will try and copy and steal your product, and a number will be interested in buying the company outright.

Large organizations find it hard to innovate and big software companies are no different. Often for a large global technology giant, it is just easier and simpler to buy your whole business outright, than to try and build from scratch internally. This is especially true if your company is deemed to possess a "secret sauce." A companies secret sauce is the piece of its solution that looks unique to outsiders and appears hard to replicate or copy.

We have all read headlines of companies that were two years old, with hardly any revenue, and were suddenly acquired for crazy valuations. It was for their secret sauce that the buyer paid so handsomely.

Google did not pay $500 million for "Deepmind," the London Artificial Intelligence start-up (with no revenue and no near-term prospect of generating any), because they liked the name. They paid this gigantic sum for the code because it was light years ahead of the competition and would have taken Google many years to replicate.

If you do get approached about selling out, remember there are two types of acquisitions:

1. **Financial**—A company buys you at a multiple of your current revenue or EBITDA. You are never interested in this. The multiple will be small and as you have little revenue yet, so will be the corresponding price they are prepared to pay.

2. **Strategic**—A company buys you for synergy, that is, to grow the business massively within their umbrella and using the huge financial firepower they possess (and you don't). In this instance, a company might want your intellectual property and use their deep pockets to scale growth globally, at their international client base. They will often pay a high price for your "secret sauce," as they are buying the **potential** of your business, not your current book of business.

Either way, it pays to start conversations early with the key potential acquirers in your industry and also the main M&A advisory companies that focus on your space. The companies that may acquire you are often potential interim business partners, whereas M&A agencies work with the corporate development departments of large global businesses. They are keen to find fast growing, exciting technology companies to assist their clients' strategic expansion.

Remember, your VC investors will want an exit from the business. Either through the company being acquired or at a later financing round when they are "bought out." Having your "secret sauce" in great shape going into the Series A will help maximize company valuation. Having discussions with potential acquisition partners will impress VCs and generate enhanced investor interest.

Chapter Summary

- Constant innovation is the only way to stay ahead of your competition

- Have your clients sponsor innovation and development of your product roadmap.

- Innovation drives the company's valuation and makes fundraising easier.

- You must have a "secret sauce" to justify a high valuation, for both fundraising and acquisition purposes.

- Never accept a "financial" acquisition offer.

- You are only ever potentially interested in a "strategic" acquisition offer.

CHAPTER 15

Securing a Series A Funding Round

Understanding Series A Capital

Series A funding is scaling capital. It is that simple.

Let's recap here:

Your angel investor backed you when no one else would.

Your seed round enabled you to prove the product, sign up a few more clients and line up a nice pipeline of larger prospects.

Series A funding is **the cash you need to deliver them**. Copy and repeat. Copy and repeat some more. That's how you turn your business into a "Unicorn."

Many, many companies go bust between angel and seed funding. A whole lot more go bust between seed and Series A funding. Once you have made it to Series A, ironically, you actually have a far higher chance of reaching Series B—essentially turning your $10 million Series A valuation into a Series B $100 million company.

At the Series A funding point, it is all about scaling up globally, putting repeatable processes in place, bringing home fast-growing revenue and repeat, if required, for more funding.

Sounds easy right? Of course, it's not.

It is still immensely difficult to scale properly, but at least with your Series A in the bag, you will have a more robust runway in place and a larger war chest to deliver it.

The Series A round is the point at which hiring—and correspondingly the wider business expenses—will **really** start to ramp up. For a first-time entrepreneur or founder, this can be a shock.

In the early days, you were probably aghast at spending $5,000 per month. That $50,000 from your angel seemed like a fortune that would last forever. Then the seed round came along, and you start to expand. The world seems your oyster. Then all of a sudden, you are burning through tens of thousands of dollars per month. Well now, after Series A, the company will likely be spending hundreds of thousands of dollars a month.

The Series A Shortage

To be in with a decent chance of nailing a Series A funding round, you need to have projected revenue over the next year of at least $1 million (some would say more). This figure has waxed and waned over the years, as the size of funding checks have grown and shrank with the economic cycle.

Fundraising for Series A is a bit of a chicken and egg scenario. You will find it hard to reach $1 million or $2 million in revenue with the funding from your seed round alone, and the small size of the team means it is hard to close huge multi-six figure deals. The way round this is to have **some excellent growth from the seed round and some well advanced, big prospects coming down your sales pipeline**, that will deliver huge revenue growth. That story will make sense to Series A investors.

You will basically be at the point where you can't grow quickly anymore. If you don't raise a Series A, you will miss out on these larger, more lucrative deals. You won't have the funding or credibility in place to hire the great team you need to scale the business and win the industry titans.

Luckily, VCs understand this. As many have been entrepreneurs themselves, they know a technology company starts to tread water when it runs out of scaling capital. That you start to leave deals and money on the table because you simply don't have the funding to chase them or the resources to deliver them. That's a lot of valuation and revenue growth that's been left behind. Once you have a firm pipeline in place and a few good reference clients behind you, VCs will understand it's time to inject the real scaling capital.

One factor that does complicate things is that **there is less Series A funding around** than there should be. At this point, you need investors to make a material commitment. Ideally $2 or $3 million, perhaps even as much as $5 million.

VC and angel funding are often clumped **at either end of the start-up journey**. In other words, there are loads of investors out there that can write a check for $250,000, and possibly up to a million dollars. These guys make a small bet on you, while they see if you can get some traction and build on the first client. At the other end of the scale, there are also plenty of VCs who will happily stick hundreds of millions or even billions, into any of the mature tech unicorns we all know well.

What's **missing is in the middle**. The scaling capital you need to start expanding properly globally. You require too much money from the seed VCs. The check you need is too large for their investment diversification. They want to make smaller punts on a large portfolio of start-ups.

For the large VCs, **you are still too risky and unproven** in the market. Plus, the few million dollars you will need is too small for them to put to work. They won't fund a scaling technology company that doesn't have global recognition (i.e., you are not Airbnb or Uber). Their minimum investment is probably far north of $20 million anyway.

This leaves a **shortage of Series A investors** to provide the scaling capital you require.

The way to overcome this is by **building great investor relationships.**

How to Find the Money

Finding your Series A funding is quite different from sourcing your seed round. At the seed stage, most investors had never heard of you or your company. By the time you get to Series A, the VCs in your space **will know you** or at least something about the business.

This makes it easier in one sense to get meetings and start a decent conversation. On the other hand, it means they will drill you on your past performance, traction since the seed round, and the pipeline you need to deliver, if they fund your Series A.

For Series A, the VC "spray gun" approach that you may have used for the seed round does not work. Finding a lead VC investor for your Series A is a **sniper shoot**. You should focus relentlessly on the VC you want to "lead" your round and pour the lion's share of VC engagement into that one firm.

You notice I said, **lead investor**. That's on purpose. At Series A level, a round is often led by one VC and then followed at smaller amounts by a number of others. That might mean your lead would chip in $1 million and four other VCs will put in $250,000 each. It doesn't always work this way, but it's more common than not.

You will still have a decent VC rolodex from pounding the pavements for your seed round. It pays to keep in touch with these guys, even if they didn't invest and send them updates from time to time, especially when you reach key milestones or any important business wins.

For the Series A, working on developing existing VC contacts is the best way to start. Even if they don't want to invest or don't look at Series A funding, they will know the right VC firms to introduce you to. A **warm recommendation** from one VC to another, is a great place to start your discussions.

Start sending prospective Series A investors **quarterly updates of your "Investment Summary,"** so that they can see the progress you are making—both as a company and as a return for your earlier investors (i.e., the company valuation is increasing quickly). Talk to them regularly on their fundraising and investment strategies. What money are they raising? Where are they in that process? How much firepower is left in their fund to be put to work and what is their timeline for investing? You need to cultivate a real relationship. Get to know them well and it will really pay off when you need to raise this large round. Even tell them a few true "war stories" where things didn't work out. They will appreciate the honesty. Tell them that if you had had the funding in place, it would have made a difference. It's your way of turning a weakness into a strength.

Perhaps a VC that passed over your seed round can sometimes be convinced to come into the Series A. This happens all the time. Especially if you have performed well in the interim. The ideal scenario is that your Series A is led—or at least contributed to—by your seed VC.

While it is probably unlikely that your seed VC would also lead the Series A, if this happens, it makes everything much easier. Other VCs will be extremely impressed that the seed VC is **investing again at a higher valuation**. That is unusual, so when it happens, it's a sign of real credibility—as the seed VC is putting their money where their mouth is.

In addition, if the seed VC is leading the Series A round, then all the original investment documentation can be updated quickly and the whole deal can be turned around in a couple of months, rather than a couple of quarters.

Your **original seed VC can be invaluable in helping with the Series A** fundraise. Relentlessly push them to introduce you to their investor network. Also, have them **join the first calls/meetings with potential Series A investors**. While you do your pitch, have them sing your praises as a future Unicorn and the best investment they ever made.

VCs are incredibly herd-like and if your seed VC is talking about what a great company you are and how much they love working with you, you are halfway home to finding a decent Series A lead. The seed VC should emphasize the great value you have created, with a small amount of seed funding. Imagine what you could do with a few million dollars?

The seed VC needs to tell the Series A prospect that they are looking seriously at coming in on the new funding round (or better still, that they definitely are). The fact that your original VC will buy more shares at a higher valuation, is a great vote of confidence in you and the delivery of your strategy.

Lastly, if you have done a favorable bridge funding round, now is the time to talk about it. If it was six months after your seed round and the valuation was (say) 50 percent higher, that's great. If it was 100 percent higher than your seed, then that's incredible. Having your seed VC talk about all the unrealized gains you have made for them, in this short period of time, will have larger investors salivating to be involved.

Half a dozen calls like this, working hand in hand with your seed investor, will go a long way in identifying the interested potential lead Series A VC.

You may have to do a **Dog and Pony** show in a couple of major business centers. This is where you will do live one-on-one pitches behind closed doors to a small, select number of interested investors. By now you are a pitch pro, so this shouldn't be much of an issue for you. Sometimes this can take the form of a business event or an industry dinner, but it is best if you already know the VC in question, do a rollicking presentation, fully answer their questions, and then have dinner together. Remember, it's a relationship you are building.

However way you do it, you will certainly have to spend some time physically face to face with your Series A VC. They will want to meet you in person, a number of times and have dinner, multiple business meetings, and get to know how you and your management team really tick.

After completing the standard due diligence on you and the company, the VC you end up working with, will put together a valuation of the business and a Term Sheet for the Series A round. This is an inexact science and you should have some sort of input into the process. The final number needs to be at least $10 million, as you will need a Series A round of $2+ million to be able to scale properly.

The valuation will look at your historical performance, the strategy for growth, the quality of the team you have in place and the expected future growth of the industry you are selling into. It will also laser focus on two key areas:

- The **rate of growth** the funding would allow your company to achieve over the next two years (i.e., until you may need a further injection of funding). They will also look at how fast you have grown over the last year (i.e., how efficiently you used the seed funding).
- Your **revenue "run rate" over the next twelve months.** This is the projected revenue scheduled to come in over the next year and is mainly composed of contracts you have signed and revenue that you will receive in the year ahead. It will also take a hard look at your business development pipeline and assign a probability to converting strong leads into actual sales.

For example, if you have contractual revenue of $500,000 next year and you are chasing another $1 million from deals you expect to close, the VC will probably reach a projected run rate of $1 million. This takes account of the deals that would convert and other successful opportunities yet to find. For a technology company, that would equate to a valuation of around $10 million.

In Series A, you are likely to be **selling 20 percent of the business** to the VCs and they will most likely want Convertible Preference Shares (or perhaps offer you a Convertible Loan Note). This will probably leave you as a founder with somewhere in between 30 percent and 40 percent of the company (depending on whether you had a cofounder). That figure will depend on how much you gave to the early angel and seed investors (probably about a third of the business in total) and also how much you carved out (just before the seed round) to set up the Employee Share Option Pool (likely between 5 percent and 15 percent).

"Herding the Cats"

Remember there will probably be a lead Series A investor and also a number of smaller participants, ideally including your seed VC and any historical angels. It is **much easier** to get a Series A round filled out when you have a strong lead VC. The due diligence required by the smaller investors is often much less. They sometimes depend on the lead VCs detailed analysis of the company and can often decide quickly.

For you as the CEO, managing the investment process with all these VCs is a major "herding the cats" project and quite a difficult process. Logistically, a Series A round is often five times the hassle of the seed round. Have someone you trust on the team help you get the paperwork in order and documents signed, as well as all the logistical details required to get the deal over the line.

Have them update you every few days and move quickly to address any roadblocks. These might include investors changing their mind, varying the amount they want to contribute or delays to their funding timeline. This will happen for sure during the Series A process and it's extremely frustrating and a source of many sleepless nights. You will have already begun your scaling and hiring strategy, but you need the funds in the bank to pull the trigger.

By now, you understand key VC legal terms, so it makes that legal document review process less painful. You will have some good investor management experience by now too. This is all great exposure—even most successful senior businesspeople never learn how to manage a group of professional investors.

Unfortunately, the Series A process is still pretty painful, and like the seed round, takes up an inordinate amount of time.

It is also an excellent time to have removed anything you didn't like in the **original investment agreement**. For example, the seed investment agreement may have had restrictive covenants on what you, as the CEO, could do with the money (e.g., borrow on the company's behalf). There could also be personal restrictions on founder shares too, including having them locked up and requiring VCs approval for any sale or transfer. Now is the time to have them reviewed and removed. It's also traditionally the time an initial shareholder or founder who wants to move on or doesn't share your scaling vision, is bought out from the company.

Building Your Series A Team

You now need to hire or promote into place, a reliable top tier management team. The team will sit below you to run the business day to day, while you drive the strategy and come in at the right time, to shake the hand of your latest customer.

These **three or four trusted lieutenants** will manage the operational, product, technology, and business development teams. They are highly likely to be at least some of the original team that came with you on the journey over the last few years. They will have the experience, knowledge, and appetite to keep scaling the business.

Perhaps you or the investors want to **recruit externally**. This can be a great time to find amazing talent. The business finally has some real funding firepower, new share options may be available, and the company should have the reputation to land a couple of real experts in your industry. If you are concerned that too much senior new blood could negatively impact the original team, instead hire senior sales staff to focus on **international markets**.

From your perspective, around this time, you should have a clear idea which trusted lieutenant could take over the CEO position in the future. Post Series A, the board of directors will want a clear succession plan in place, should you happen to fall ill, resign, or get hit by a bus.

If none of them are suitable for this role, then look outside the company and find a number two externally. It will take time, so move slowly and don't rush this important process. Having a suitable number two in place is something many start-up CEOs never do. It is a sign of their ego and a symbol of bad planning. A well-run company, setting its sight on global domination, needs an executable succession plan in place.

What Do You Do Now?

Now that you have a team that manages the day to day and a company valued in eight figures and is fully funded for the next couple of years, you have an important question to ask yourself.

What do I do now?

Speak to a professional business coach who will help you take a cold hard look at your skill set.

The requirements of a scaling CEO **are different** from that of a start-up CEO. Growing a business post Series A is a different skill set than setting up a new company. Do you have it?

Do not become a barrier to the growth of your own business. Too many start-up CEOs make this mistake. Do not be one of them.

Answering the question honestly will also lead to a happier work life for you. If you do stay, **your role will change**. The company will have to put in place proper procedures and processes, the way all businesses do when they reach a certain size. The start-up "buzz" may start to fade for you, and you need to ask yourself whether you prefer **starting a business or running a business**.

You, as the CEO, will spend your time devising the strategy for the next year, working with the board and your core lieutenants on its implementation. You will speak at many events and keep talking to investors. You will be wheeled in at the last minute to "bless" a major client deal or sales relationship. You will still have to approve major changes to technology, overseas expansion, and product road plans, but you are moving further and further away from the day-to-day operations.

If this does not appeal to you, then it is time to think about **moving on**.

This can be done in a number of ways. By the time a company completes a Series A round, many founders can be five years into their big adventure, and they are ready to do something else. Many of them join or even head up the board of directors. They often stay around in an advisory capacity, to help out the new CEO that had been appointed.

That handover process to your number two can typically take six months or more. It **can't be rushed**. The investors won't allow that. Clients will want assurances that you will still be involved, and as the founder, provide some sort of overview or insight into the business.

By stepping into a **senior advisory role,** you can accomplish this and still be involved in the company to a degree that makes you happy. You can be involved, but not responsible.

If the business is not fun anymore, if you find yourself daydreaming about walking away or doing something else (or if your partner does), then this is the time to hand over the reins to your number two.

Conclusion

Remember, by the time of a Series A round, you have learned more than what 99% of people ever experience about entrepreneurship. You will have amassed not just an immense amount of business knowledge, but also critical business experience. Very few start-up CEOs make it this far and your skills and experience are eminently applicable to starting or supporting other start-up businesses.

Chapter Summary

- Have your original VC introduce you to Series A investors.
- Push your seed VC hard to commit to reinvesting in the Series A round.
- Series A VCs are found on a relationship basis. A recommendation from your seed VC works wonders.
- Laser focus on specific Lead Series A investor and then work hard to get them to commit to at least $1 million.
- The remainder of the Series A round can be filled much faster once a reputable lead is in place.
- Appoint a trusted member of your staff to help herd the cats and manage the logistics.
- Aim for a Pre-Money Valuation of at least $10 million.
- Use the Series A investment agreement to buy out any original shareholders/founders that want to exit.
- Consider if you want to stay for the next phase of growth or handover to a professional CEO to scale the company.

CHAPTER 16

Conclusion

It must be considered that there is nothing more difficult to carry out nor more doubtful of success nor more dangerous to handle than to initiate a new order of things.

Niccolo Machiavelli (1469–1527)

You have grown a $10+ million business from nothing but an idea in your head. That is an incredible achievement.

You now have to decide if you wish to stay on board and drive the next stage of growth and worldwide expansion. Perhaps you do or maybe you don't. Either way, try and take some time to stand back and celebrate everything you have achieved. Of the half million companies that are created each month in the United States, less than a few thousand annually will ever successfully raise Series A funding.

Many entrepreneurs enjoy the exciting start-up phase of growing a company. Pulling together the initial team and having the product built. Getting that first client over the line and the seed funding deal in the bag. Many do not enjoy the actual day to day of running the company. I count myself amongst that group.

For people like me, we tend to look at exciting new projects, while becoming senior advisors to the companies we founded, mentoring the newly appointed CEO on business strategy, and acting as a sounding board for growth and client acquisition.

Whatever you decide to do next, the entrepreneurial expertise you will have acquired over the last few years is invaluable. You can use this knowledge to set up a new business, advise other small companies or even help large organizations with their innovation strategy.

This book has been intended as a practical guide for company founders who wish to reach an eight-figure valuation and Series A funding.

To put some structure around the key steps and milestones required to reach a valuation in excess of $10 million. I wanted to demystify the whole process and make it clearly achievable to anyone with a great idea, bags of persistence, and enough resilience to make it a reality.

It took me five years, from forming my technology company, to receiving a Series A Term Sheet. I wish this book had existed when I was starting out. It would have saved me at least two years, going down the wrong road, approaching the wrong prospects, and going round in circles, trying to raise capital.

I had never run a technology company before. I had no idea how to raise institutional capital. The legal terms mystified me and selling to large organizations frightened me. On the way, I made many mistakes, endured deep personal tragedy, and flirted many times with bankruptcy.

But I got there in the end.

You can too.

About the Author

Shane Brett is one of Europe's leading FinTech entrepreneurs.

He has created multiple technology companies and consultancies globally and personally raised over $3.5 million from leading institutional and VC investors in the United States, Europe, Abu Dhabi, and APAC.

Shane has directly created over U.S. $12 million in value for early stage institutional seed investors—including doubling one FinTech valuation in 8 months—and then again 6 months later.

He has successfully scaled technology businesses globally including into New York, London, Lisbon, and Sydney, as well as building and selling pioneering blockchain compliance technology into some of the world's largest fund management firms.

In 2016 one of the technology companies he founded won Europe's largest start up competition.

Shane has written three business & technology books and dozens of technology news articles, peer reviewed academic articles and industry white papers. He has been featured in the Financial Times, NASDAQ, Reuters, Forbes & the Irish Times.

Shane has 25 years' experience in investment funds and emerging technology and has worked in senior roles or consulted for BNP Paribas, HSBC Securities Services, Northern Trust, UBS & Aberdeen Asset Management, in Dublin, London, Edinburgh, New York and Sydney.

As well as being a Founding Member of The International RegTech Association (IRTA) and speaking regularly at some of the largest technology conferences in the world. Shane also worked closely for many years with the world's leading global regulators, including the Irish Central Bank, FCA (UK), SEC (USA & ASIC (Australia).

Shane coach's technology entrepreneurs around the world and advises technology companies how to scale and grow their businesses successfully.

Index

www.ingramcontent.com/pod-product-compliance
Lightning Source LLC
Chambersburg PA
CBHW061312220326
41599CB00026B/4844